Norman Rockwell's
Chronicles of America

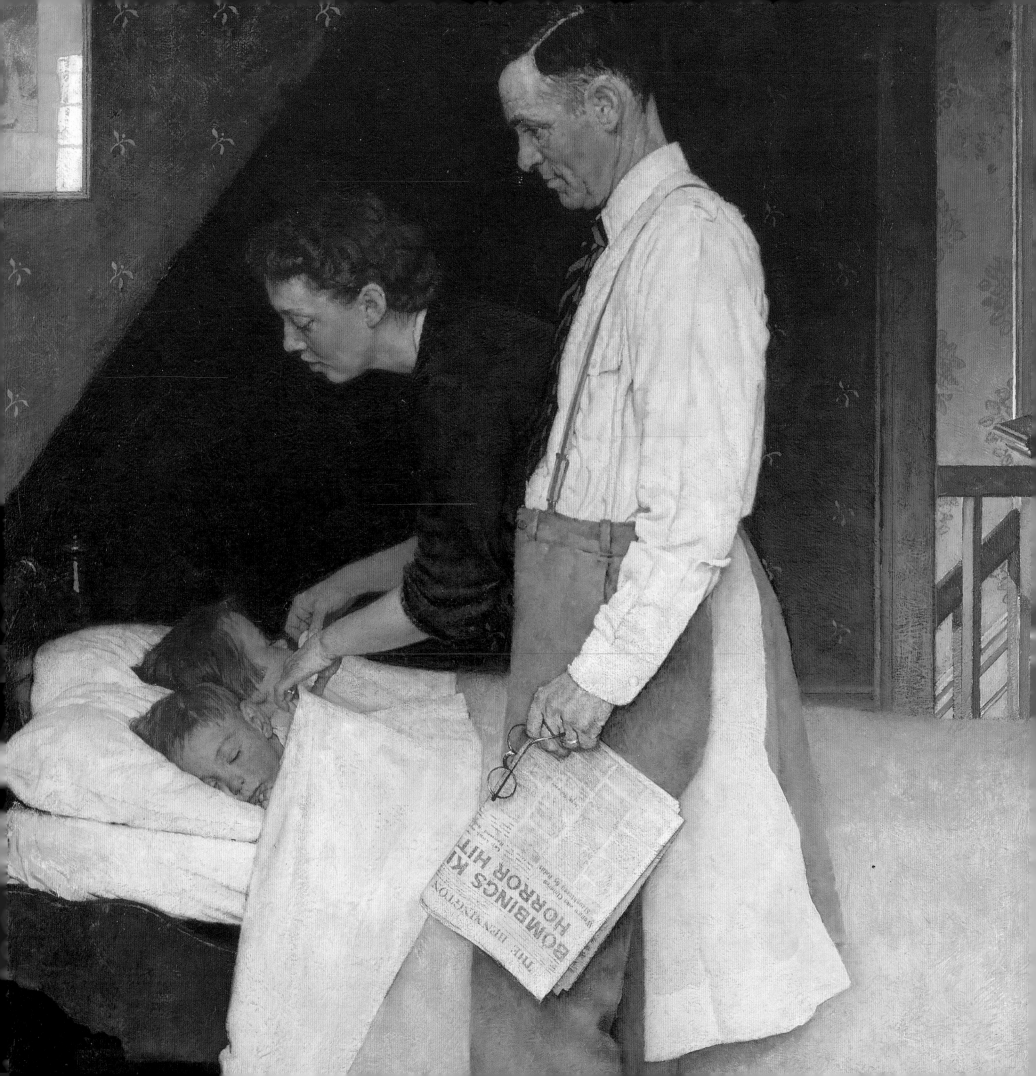

THE BENNINGTON
BOMBINGS KI
HORROR HIT

Norman Rockwell's
Chronicles of America

MARGARET T. ROCKWELL

BARNES
&NOBLE
BOOKS
NEW YORK

This edition published by Barnes & Noble, Inc.
by arrangement with Michael Friedman Publishing Gorup, Inc.

1998 Barnes & Noble Books

ISBN 0-7607-0961-0

M 10 9 8 7 6 5 4 3 2 1

Editor: Nathaniel Marunas
Art Director: Lynne Yeamans
Designer: Joseph Rutt
Photography Director: Christopher C. Bain
Production Associate: Camille Lee

Color separations by Fine Arts Repro House Co., Ltd.
Printed in China by Leefung-Asco Printers Ltd.

Dedication

To Geoffrey, Peter, and Thea with love

Acknowledgments

Heartfelt thanks to Dana Legassie of Dictaphone Canada and
to Tom Rockwell for his encouragement and guidance.

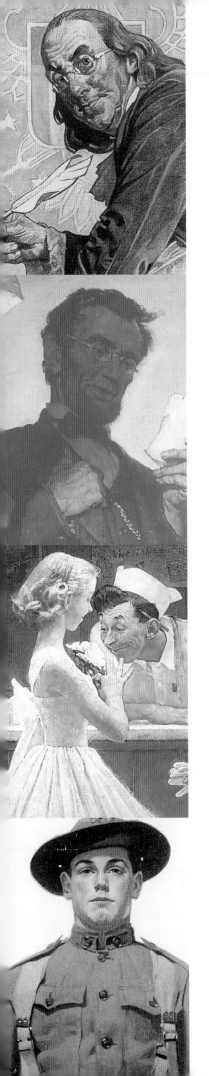

Contents

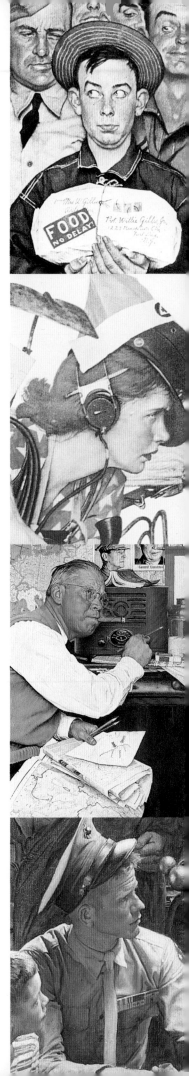

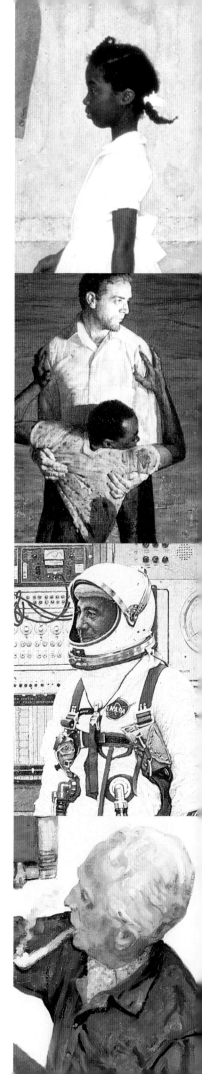

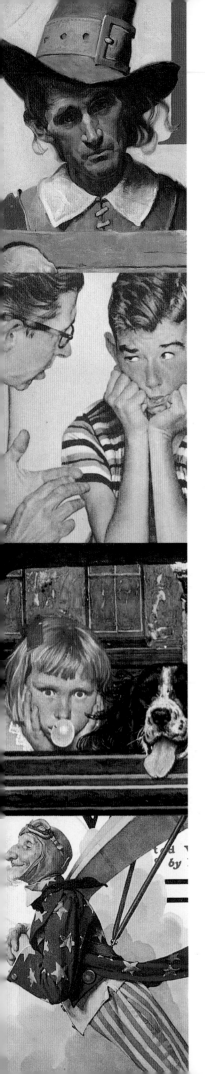

INTRODUCTION

During his lifetime, Norman Rockwell produced more than four thousand illustrations. These paintings and drawings were used for magazine covers, commercial advertisements, and story illustrations. The images reflected his times, sometimes representing the world as Rockwell and his audience preferred to see it. His paintings depict the customs, lifestyles, and pre-occupations of American society for a major part of the twentieth century. Seen chronologically they tell of a changing world, showing boys in knickerbockers at play, young men going to war, women going to work, Americans dying in the fight for civil rights, and hu-mankind at large accomplishing things that only a cen-tury before had seemed impossible.

Norman Rockwell was born in 1894. When he started painting he himself was still wearing the knee-length pants worn by youths of that era. He finally put down his brush as an old man, having as a boy ridden in an early automobile and more recently witnessed the moon landing. Rockwell died in 1978.

The sampling of paintings presented in this book tell the story of an artist's development and a country's growth. The paintings are divided into four chapters that contain brief biographical accounts of Rockwell's life. Common themes are identified, discussed, and often enriched with comments made by Rockwell himself concerning his work and the changing times he lived through.

CHAPTER ONE
Early Ambitions

1894-1929

Norman Rockwell was born on February 3, 1894, in an apartment on 103rd Street and Amsterdam Avenue in New York City. His parents, Nancy and Waring Rockwell, had one older boy, Jarvis, who was a year and a half Norman's senior. Rockwell considered his older brother to be a fabulous athlete, strong and fearless—a "boy's boy"—while he saw himself as skinny, bespectacled, and not at all athletic. Rockwell's ability to draw, however, gave him a special status among his boyhood friends.

The family lived in New York City until Rockwell was nine years old, at which point they moved to the suburban commuter town of Mamaroneck, New York. Rockwell started high school in Mamaroneck and left in 1909, during his sophomore year, to study art in New York City. While he initially attended a number of different art schools, he settled on the Art Students League, where he studied drawing and illustration with George Bridgeman and Thomas Fogarty.

As a student Rockwell was given small illustration jobs, but his big break came in 1912 with his first book contract, to illustrate C.H. Claudy's *Tell Me Why: Stories About Mother Nature.* He considered it his first real job and marked the event by

Family Tree
Oil on canvas
46 × 42 inches
(117 × 106.5cm)
First published on the cover of
The Saturday Evening Post,
October 24, 1959

The Hike Book
"Touching a High Spot"
First published in *The Hike Book* by Edward Cave, 1913

renting his first studio. He then drew illustrations for Boy Scout handbooks on hiking and camping. The editor was pleased with the nineteen-year-old artist's work and assigned Rockwell stories to illustrate for the magazine *Boys' Life*. The young illustrator was soon made art director of *Boys' Life*. With his portfolio expanding, Rockwell was able to get work illustrating other children's magazines, such as *St. Nicholas, Everyland, American Boy,* and *Youth's Companion*.

In 1915 Rockwell and his family moved to New Rochelle, New York, where he shared a studio with Clyde Forsythe. In 1916 George Horace Lorimer, editor of *The Saturday Evening Post,* accepted two of Rockwell's paintings to appear as *Post* covers and approved three sketches for future covers. Rockwell's first *Post* cover was published in May 1916, and later that year Rockwell married Irene O'Connor. In 1918 he enlisted in the U.S. Navy and was stationed at the Naval Reserve Base in Charleston, South Carolina, where he was made art director of the camp newspaper, *Afloat and Ashore*.

During the 1920s Irene and Norman Rockwell partied with New Rochelle society. They had their own bootlegger and belonged to a country club. Rockwell traveled to Europe without Irene in 1927 and again in 1929. On his return in 1929 Irene asked him for a divorce. She had fallen in love with someone else. The high living of the Roaring Twenties was over.

Two Men Courting Girl's Favor
First published on the cover of *The Saturday Evening Post*, January 13, 1917

YANKEE DOODLE CAME TO TOWN · RIDING ON A PONY · STUCK A FEATHER IN HIS HAT · AND CALLED IT MACARONI

TOP:
Yankee Doodle
Oil on canvas
60 × 152 inches (152.5 × 386cm)
First used as a wall mural for Nassau Inn, 1937

ABOVE:
Approaching Ships
Used as an early book illustration, 1911

Painting American History

One of Rockwell's first illustration assignments was for an American history book. At only seventeen years of age, he was asked to draw Samuel de Champlain, the explorer of the St. Lawrence River, for the American Book Company. He used his father as a model for the explorer. Still perfecting his illustration technique, Rockwell was unable to make the water of the St. Lawrence look far enough below the high ramparts of Quebec City. This would be the first of many depictions of events in North American history painted by Rockwell.

Rockwell's great hero was Howard Pyle, a famous American illustrator who strove to achieve historical accuracy in his illustrations. Rockwell described Pyle as "a historian with a brush" and attempted to paint like him. Pyle lived through what Rockwell called "the golden age of illustration" and died while Rockwell was still in art school.

Rockwell enjoyed painting figures in period costumes and frequently painted nostalgic covers for the *Post* through the 1920s and up until the mid-1930s. He painted the "Yankee Doodle" mural depicting a colonial scene for the Nassau Inn in Princeton, New Jersey, in 1937. Although he loved to paint the swirling scarlet capes, the lace collars, and the pantaloons with frills, he stopped painting them because he feared the costume paintings had lost their appeal. In the early years of his career, people identified with the past and felt connected to the nineteenth century, but as time progressed he grew concerned that people were finding it increasingly difficult to relate to the characters in the costume paintings.

Rockwell had an extensive collection of colonial costumes, uniforms, old guns, and antiques that he used as props for the costume pictures. Unfortunately, most of his collection was lost when his studio burned down in 1943.

In his book on how to draw, *Rockwell on Rockwell: How I Make a Picture,* Rockwell emphasized the importance of good research in order to make a painting look authentic when depicting an historic event. Before he painted Lincoln giving the Gettysburg address, he'd read that the speech was given in the late afternoon—therefore, the painting required a long shadow. He learned that Lincoln wore a double-breasted frock coat and carried a gold watch on a chain. He also discovered that Lincoln's entire address had been written on two scraps of crumpled paper. Rockwell painted the other figures in the painting from old prints and used a model who specialized in Lincoln portrayals. All this gave him the confidence to paint as authentic-looking a painting as possible.

In 1963 Rockwell illustrated Benjamin Franklin's *Poor Richard's Almanack* for Heritage Press. Rockwell chose to illustrate several historic episodes from Franklin's life in color and thirty-six of Franklin's sayings with small pen-and-ink drawings, which were distributed throughout the book. These illustrations are reminiscent of the colonial pieces Rockwell drew earlier in his career.

Yankee Doodle
Oil on canvas
36 × 27 inches (91.5 × 68.5cm)
First used as a study for "Yankee Doodle," a wall mural for Nassau Inn, 1937

TOP LEFT:
Poor Richard's Almanack
  "Drive thy Business!—let not it drive you"
Pen and ink on paper
4 × 4 inches (10 × 10cm)
First published in *Almanacks*, 1963

TOP RIGHT:
Poor Richard's Almanack
  "A good Wife and Health, is a Man's best Wealth"
Pen and ink on paper
4 × 4 inches (10 × 10cm)
First published in *Almanacks*, 1963

RIGHT:
Poor Richard's Almanack
  *"Tim was so learned, that he could name a Horse in nine
  Languages. So ignorant, that he bought a cow to ride on."*
Pen and ink on paper
4 × 4 inches (10 × 10cm)
First published in *Almanacks*, 1963

Ben Franklin's Sesquicentennial
Oil on canvas
38 × 28 inches (96.5 × 71cm)
First published on the cover of *The
Saturday Evening Post*, May 29, 1926

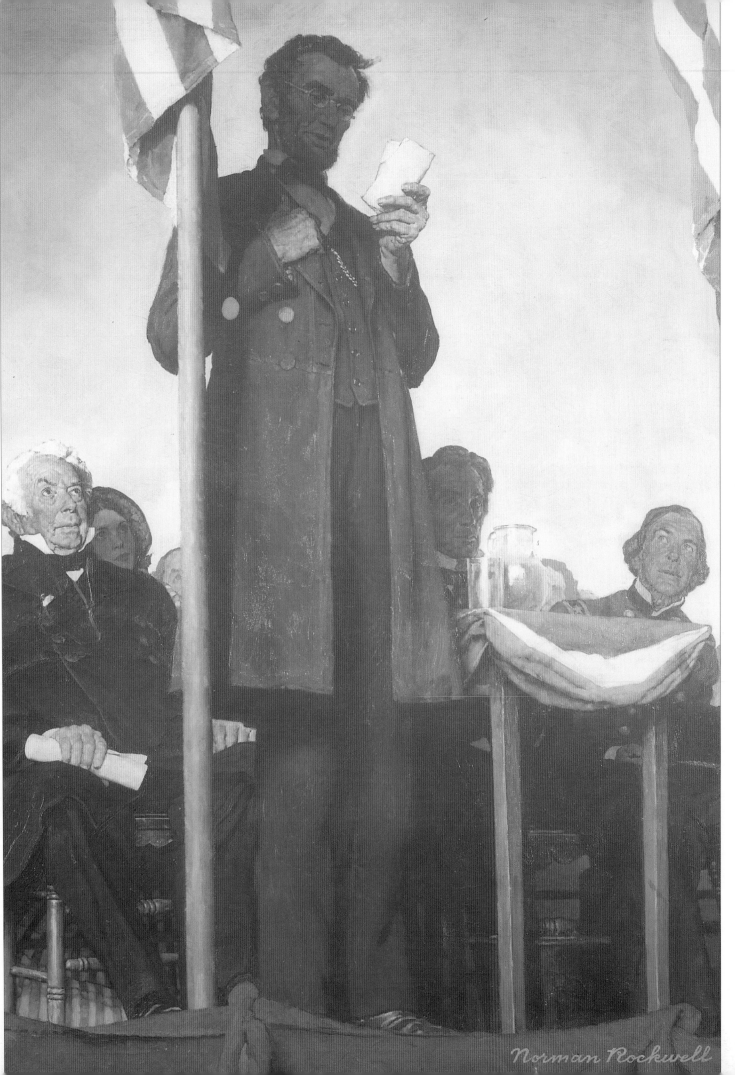

**Abraham Lincoln
Delivering the
Gettysburg Address**
Oil on canvas
49.5 × 36 inches
(125 × 91.5cm)
First published in *McCall's*,
July 1942

RIGHT:
Tell Me Why
*"Then Mother Nature woke up Bear,
and Bear woke up what other animals
he could find...."*
Used in *Tell Me Why*, 1912

BELOW:
The Red Arrow
*"The spirit of the chase has seized him, and
he rode recklessly into the great company of
crowding buffaloes."*
Oil on canvas
20 × 32 inches (51 x 81cm)
Used to illustrate Elmer Russell Gregor's
Red Arrow, 1915

Colonial Couple under Mistletoe
First published on the cover of
The Saturday Evening Post,
December 19, 1936

Milkmaid
Oil on canvas
30.75 × 23 inches (78 × 58cm)
First published on the cover of The
    Saturday Evening Post, July 25, 1931

Thanksgiving—Ye Glutton
(*also* Pilgrim in Stockade)
Oil on canvas
31 × 22 inches (79 × 59cm)
First published on the cover of *Life*,
November 22, 1923

Pipe and Bowl Sign Painter
Oil on canvas
26.5 × 21.75 inches (67 × 55cm)
First published on the cover of
The Saturday Evening Post,
February 6, 1926

Painting Children

Rockwell painted children from the very beginning. As a student at the Art Students League, he was awarded a scholarship to Thomas Fogarty's class for producing the best illustration. It was a black-and-white charcoal drawing entitled "The Fourth of July." It featured a little boy sick in bed with the mumps, a kerchief tied around his head, while outside the window fireworks are exploding. As Rockwell once pointed out, the painting was very similar to the work he did throughout the rest of his career.

Rockwell's early years as a professional illustrator were almost entirely devoted to children's magazines. At nineteen years of age, he was drawing subjects that were certain to interest young boys in the early twentieth century: adventure, heroic rescues, wilderness, American Indians, and sports figures. Eventually, however, he wanted to do illustrations for a more widely read publication, and he sought advice and encouragement from his studio-mate and good friend Clyde Forsythe.

Well, I wanted to advance my work....I was making so little money for children's magazines. [Forsythe] encouraged me because he had a lot of courage being a newspaperman. At that time, the thing to do for an illustrator was to paint a Saturday Evening Post *cover. 'So,' he said, 'Why don't you do one?' Gee, I was only twenty-one and I thought, gee, I can't do a* Post *cover. He was all for encouraging me to do it, so I started one. I had almost a kind of Gibson picture: a Gibson girl, a beautiful girl in evening clothes on a couch with a beautiful young man leaning over her about to kiss her and so on. Of course I hadn't been brought up in that kind of society and I didn't know really how it looked but I got a model with a tuxedo and a beautiful girl in evening clothes and they posed. I got about halfway through it. I was discouraged because it didn't look high class. And then he said, 'Why don't you do things with kids in them? Why don't you do the kind of thing you do for* Boys' Life, St. Nicholas *and so on.' So, gee, I thought that might be a pretty good idea....I started on it. Right away I found I could paint it because this was the kind of thing I'd been doing for kids' magazines....I'd done so many children and evidently had a knack for it.*

Rockwell's first *Saturday Evening Post* cover was of a young boy dressed in a tie, a jacket, and a fastened-on derby hat, pushing a baby carriage past two of his mocking friends, who are off to play baseball. The baby's mother has placed a

OPPOSITE:
Boy with Baby Carriage
Oil on canvas
20.75 × 18.625 inches (53 × 47cm)
First published on the cover of *The Saturday Evening Post*, May 20, 1916

BELOW:
Little Girl Working for Red Cross
First published on the cover of *The Saturday Evening Post*, September 21, 1918

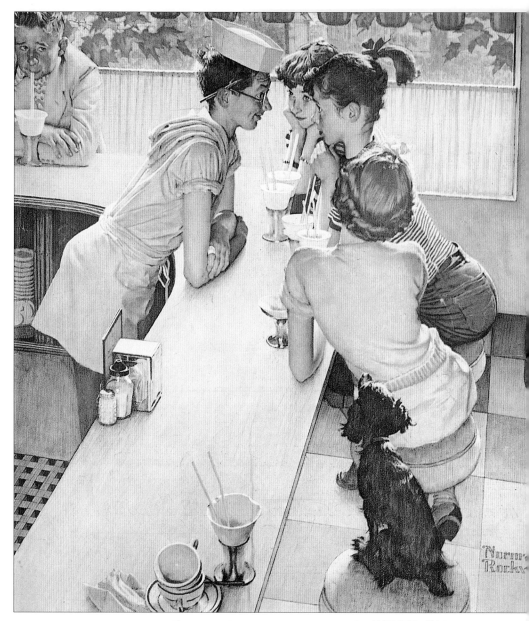

ABOVE:
After the Prom
Oil on canvas
31 × 29 inches (79 × 73.5cm)

ABOVE:
Soda Jerk
Oil on canvas
36 × 34 inches (91.5 × 86.5cm)
First published on the cover of *The Saturday
    Evening Post*, August 22, 1953

OPPOSITE:
Boy in a Dining Car
Oil on canvas
38 × 36 inches (96.5 × 91.5cm)
First published on the cover of *The Saturday
    Evening Post*, December 7, 1946

Norman Rockwell

Facts of Life
Oil on canvas
44 × 33.5 inches (112 × 85cm)
First published on the cover of
The Saturday Evening Post,
July 14, 1951

bottle in the babysitter's jacket pocket with the nipple peeking out of the top, adding to the poor boy's humiliation. This painting was published as the cover of the May 20, 1916, issue of the *Post*.

Children dominated the work of Rockwell's early years as a cover artist. He painted them as carefree and fun-loving youngsters. The boys were either country boys with bare feet or city boys with lace-up leather shoes. His boys wore dungarees on the farm, and in more formal situations they wore stiff collars, jackets, knee-length pants, and stockings with reinforced knees. Children were shown with dance cards and party crackers, and on occasion attempting to spell "Peloponnesus."

To encourage his young models to hold the pose while he painted them, Rockwell stacked nickels on a table beside his easel. After every twenty-five-minute period, when it was time for the model to rest, he'd transfer five nickels to the child's pile. This way the child could see his pile grow as the session proceeded and feel compensated for keeping still. Rockwell used pennies for younger children so that their piles were bigger and would grow faster. When he began to take photographs of his models in the latter half of the 1930s he was able to get more elaborate and difficult poses from the children.

During the First World War, he painted what he thought European children would look like gratefully greeting the American doughboys. During the Second World War, Rockwell focused on the adult civilian scene, returning more frequently to depictions of children after the conflict was over. When he did depict children during the 1940s, his own boys were used as models—as were many of the other children of Arlington, Vermont.

Norman Rockwell's view of childhood didn't really change through the years. Instead, the situations changed. For instance, the stockings and the stiff collars were eventually abandoned, but the boys themselves remained the same: they loved their dogs, playing baseball, running, and swimming. They disliked school, taking medicine, and keeping tidy. Rockwell's girls, on the other hand, did change. In the early years girls were presented as passive targets of boyish affection. In 1939, however, Rockwell began to reflect society's evolving attitudes by painting a marble champion with a ponytail and wearing a dress. Girls became more independent over the years: in 1953 Rockwell painted his favorite model, Mary Whalen, sporting a victor's smile and a black eye as she sits outside the principal's office.

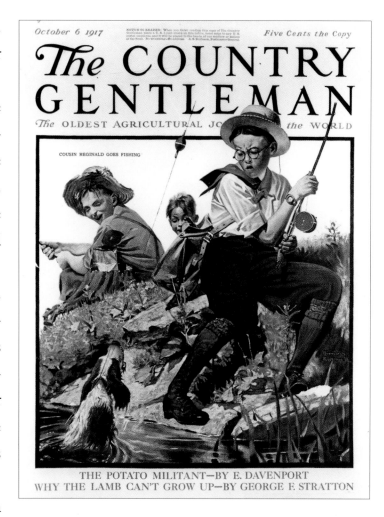

Cousin Reginald
Charcoal on posterboard
9.5 × 8.5 inches (24 × 21.5cm)
First published on the cover of
The Country Gentleman,
October 6, 1917

OPPOSITE:
Girl with a Black Eye
Oil on canvas
36 × 30 inches
    (86 × 76cm)
First published on the
    cover of *The Saturday
    Evening Post*, May 23,
    1953

RIGHT:
Prom Dress
First published on the
    cover of *The Saturday
    Evening Post*, March 19,
    1949

LEFT:
Saying Grace
Oil on canvas
42 × 40 inches (107 × 102cm)
First published on the cover of
The Saturday Evening Post,
November 24, 1951

OPPOSITE:
Breaking Home Ties
(*also* Boy and Father
Sitting on Truck)
Oil on canvas
First published on the cover of
The Saturday Evening Post,
September 25, 1954

The Country Life

Rockwell's early illustrations depicted the joys of a carefree country life, reflecting Rockwell's perception that farm life was idyllic. He developed this view during his early childhood, when he played in the dirty back alleys and abandoned lots of New York City. In the summer his family would leave the city to stay in a farmhouse in the country.

We would stay all summer on this farm, where they took in boarders. This was very exciting to my brother and I. It was never drudgery. I remember Hal Jessop, the farmer's son. He hated the farm work. He hated milking cows. He hated taking the horses down to the river for a drink before the night. But to my brother and I, it was wild adventure. We just loved it all summer long. My father would come out every weekend from the city, from his job. And then he would take two weeks off and we'd go fishing and everything like that and have a wonderful time.

I remember the haymow. The wonderful fragrance of the hay, lying in the coolness of the barn—a little itchy—but so fragrant and charming compared to the city.

Then there was the hayride. The farmer would get all of us boarders on the hay wagon. My mother and father were very good singers. He was a pretty good tenor. They sang all the songs and we'd all join in. We'd go down to a band concert every Saturday night. Oh this was thrilling! It would be dark and the horses were trotting along and the smell of the hay and everybody singing together...it was all wonderful innocent fun. I thought it was absolutely glorious....

At night we'd go down to the meadow. They'd unharness the horses and we'd get up on their backs and ride them down to the river. I remember being on top of the horse. I felt like I was on Mount Everest so high up on this great big farm horse. We'd take them back to the barn and currycomb them and help bring the feed to them.

To the farm boy this was just the most awful life and all he wanted to do was to leave it and go work in a factory or go to New York and become a Wall Street man. But to me it was the most wonderful life.

Off to School
(*also* Boy and Girl on Horse)
Oil on canvas
28 × 23 inches (71 × 58.5cm)
First published on the cover of *The Literary Digest*,
    September 4, 1920

Our heaven was those months on the farm before we came back to the city. It had a lot to do with what I painted later on.

In an early series Rockwell did for the magazine *Country Gentleman,* he introduced cousin Reginald Claude Fitzhugh (page 29), a snob from the city who acts like a sissy when faced with the joys of country life. His country cousins, Rusty and Tubby Doolittle and Chuck Peterkin, and their dog, Patsy, take great delight in teasing and provoking the hapless city slicker. Rockwell would have wanted to fit in with those country cousins but he probably worried about being mistaken for the city sissy Reginald Fitzhugh. The Reginald series was introduced in August 1917 and was featured periodically on the cover of *Country Gentleman* until June 1919.

The stark dichotomy Rockwell drew between the sordid city and the idyllic country is highlighted in two paintings that were covers for *The Literary Digest* in August and November of 1920. In "Off to School," two children are riding a pony. Barefoot and fresh-faced, they appear very happy and healthy. The contrasting painting, "End of the Working Day," shows commuters heading home, making their way through a railway station. Backs bent, faces drawn, the workers are leaving their city jobs to go home to their city flats, and the entire experience looks life-draining and miserable.

Home from the County Fair
(*also* Father and Child in Carriage)
First published on the cover of *The Literary Digest,*
August 14, 1920

THE SATURDAY EVENING POST

An Illustrated Weekly
Founded A°. D! 1728 by Benj. Franklin

Vol. 193, No. 15. Published Weekly at Philadelphia. Entered as Second-Class Matter, November 18, 1879, at the Post Office at Philadelphia, Under the Act of March 3, 1879.

OCTOBER 9, 1920

5c. THE COPY
10c. in Canada

Norman Rockwell

Irvin S. Cobb — Mary Brecht Pulver — Nina Wilcox Putnam
George Pattullo — Helen Topping Miller — Samuel G. Blythe

Man and Woman Seated Back to Back
(*also* Political Argument)
First published on the cover of
The Saturday Evening Post,
October 9, 1920

Man Looking at Saxophone
(*also* Jazz It Up with a Sax)
First published on the cover of
The Saturday Evening Post,
November 2, 1929

The Automobile

Rockwell had vivid memories of his first experience with an automobile. His family had moved to the quiet commuter town of Mamaroneck in 1903. Up until then neither Rockwell nor his friends had ever ridden in a car. Only five thousand cars existed in the United States in 1904 and were sold to the rich, who would hire a chauffeur to drive them—just as they would have hired a coachman to drive their horse-drawn carriages.

Some relative, I don't think he was a direct relative, of my mother's was a chauffeur for some very wealthy people. They came up from New York and they had an automobile....He wore a chauffeur's uniform. He had brought the woman who employed him up to visit one of the estates in Mamaroneck and evidently he took the opportunity to come down and visit with my mother and bring news of her family. So he said he had to drive over to White Plains, about five or six miles [8 or 10 km] away, and would I like to go along? Well, of course, I was very excited. Gee, none of my boyfriends or anybody had ever been in an automobile before so I said oh sure I'd love to go. My mother made me go upstairs and I put on a clean shirt. I had a new little hat and I put my hat on. It was a very big car. It was an open car. It had no top on it—a very handsome big thing. And he rode up in the front and drove. For some reason or other I didn't sit up in front with him. I sat in the back. Of course there was a great roar of the motor—they must have been very noisy in those days. And much dust on the road. We started off for White Plains. Driving through Mamaroneck was sort of royal travel because all my kid friends were watching me and I was riding. It was very bouncy. You see the roads weren't good in those days. They didn't have cement roads. They had dirt roads. And I was bouncing around—a little bit of a boy—and I was trying to sit in a very dignified way with my elbow on the side of the car seat—trying to look very much at home. The boys were all waving to me and I kind of waved back in a very dignified way and we drove up to White Plains. When we started back, the motion of the car or something blew my hat off. And it was a brand new hat. This was the first time I'd ever worn it, I think. When I got back I was much impressed and very excited. I'd been for my first automobile ride. When I got out of the car, this chauffeur—I had never met him before—he said, "Didn't you have a hat?" I thought, gee, anybody who's used to a car doesn't lose his hat in a car so I lied, "Oh no, I didn't have a hat." He said, "I could have sworn you had a hat."

ABOVE:
Winter Scene and Auto
Oil on canvas
24 × 27 inches (61 × 68.5cm)
First used a tire advertisement for the Fisk Rubber
    Company, 1917

OPPOSITE:
Going and Coming
Oil on canvas
Upper canvas: 16 × 31.5 inches (40.5 × 80cm)
Lower canvas: 16 × 31.5 inches (40.5 × 80cm)
First published on the cover of *The Saturday Evening Post,*
    August 30, 1947

ABOVE:
Welcome to Elmville
(*also* Police Man Setting
Trap)
Oil on canvas
33 × 27 inches (84 × 68.5cm)
First published in *The Saturday
Evening Post*, April 20, 1929

LEFT:
The Bribe
Oil on canvas
First used as an advertisement
for Lime Crush, 1921

OPPOSITE:
Couple in Rumbleseat
Oil on board
21 × 17.25 inches (53.5 × 44cm)
First published on the cover of
The Saturday Evening Post,
July 13, 1935

As the automobile became more and more popular, changing Americans' lives forever, Rockwell made sure it appeared on his magazine covers. In the early 1920s everyone was talking about Henry Ford and his Model T, which the car maker had standardized and was marketing as "the family horse." From 1908 to 1927, fifteen million Model Ts, or Tin Lizzies (as they were known), were manufactured. A July 1920 edition of *The Saturday Evening Post* shows a family riding in their Model T with a banner hanging down the side that reads "Excuse my dust." The little Ford is picking up dust and grit and sending it back to the more substantial luxury car it is passing.

In 1924 Rockwell painted an automobile going fifteen miles per hour (24 kph). The woman passenger has her hat tied on with a kerchief and the man's derby hat is attached to his coat by a string. The driver's eyes are protected with goggles and his hand is near the horn so he can warn pedestrians ambling along the road that he is approaching at high speed.

Speed was the issue of the 1920s. An early Rockwell advertisement for Lime Crush shows a woman trying to bribe a sheriff with a bottle of the soft drink. She's obviously gone over the posted limit of fifteen miles per hour (24kph); meanwhile, the sheriff looks like he's actually considering the bribe. On a *Post* cover from 1929, Rockwell painted another policeman waiting behind a sign marking the town limits of Elmville. He's waiting, stopwatch in hand, to nab a speeder and fine him—and thereby enrich the town. Apparently there were many small American towns that were using police officers to ambush car drivers during this period, and the newspapers and car clubs complained publicly about the practice. In a 1935 *Post* cover, Rockwell shows how speed is enjoyed by some and feared by others with his depiction of a couple and their dog whizzing by in a snug rumbleseat.

A 1923 Rockwell advertisement for Overland cars presents an automobile as something unique on the road, while a painting he did for the Ford Company in the 1950s depicts a Sunday traffic jam with cars filling the canvas. He did a series of automobile advertisements for Plymouth in the early 1950s and didn't even show the product—the name was enough. Everyone understood what was involved when the little boy shouted up the stairs, "Merry Christmas, Grandma....We came in our new Plymouth." The automobile had arrived and had become a dominant part of American life.

CHAPTER TWO

A Changing World, A Developing Artist

1930–1945

As the world's economy headed into a tailspin, Norman Rockwell faced a depression of his own. His divorce from Irene O'Connor left him alone and dissatisfied. His *Post* cover of January 18, 1930, portrays America's concern with the stock exchange; when Rockwell painted this cover, he made an uncharacteristic error by showing the grocer boy leaning forward onto a third leg. Usually precise when it came to getting the image right, Rockwell didn't notice this gaffe until years later. It's a telling reminder of the stress Rockwell was experiencing in his own life.

In early 1930 Rockwell left New York City and headed to California to stay with his old friend Clyde Forsythe. Forsythe and his wife introduced Rockwell to a young schoolteacher named Mary Barstow. Rockwell was thirty-six years old, which made him fourteen years her senior. He asked her out and two weeks later he proposed. They were married on April 17, 1930. After the wedding they returned to the East to settle in New Rochelle. Their first son, Jarvis, was born in 1931. Thomas was born in 1933 and Peter in 1936.

People Reading Stock Exchange Quotations
(*also* The Common Touch)
Oil on canvas
38 × 30 inches (96.5 × 76cm)
First published on the cover of
The Saturday Evening Post,
January 18, 1930

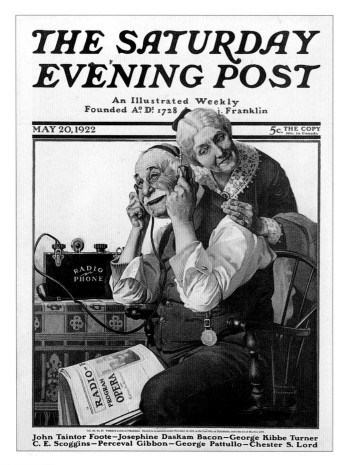

In 1938 Rockwell took his family overseas to England. The British countryside reminded Rockwell of his childhood summers outside New York City and renewed his longing for country life. On their return from England they purchased a farmhouse in Arlington, Vermont, and in 1939 the family moved in. In 1942 Rockwell painted a series of portraits called the Four Freedoms (see pages 68 to 71). *The Saturday Evening Post* published the four paintings in February and March of 1943. The paintings were used to promote the sale of war bonds and brought in more than $132,992,539. In late April 1943, Rockwell helped launch the national war-bond campaign by making a promotional appearance in Washington, D.C. Not long after his return to Arlington his studio caught fire and burned down. After the fire he and his family moved a few miles down the Batten Kill River to West Arlington's village green. Here Rockwell used a vacant one-room schoolhouse as a studio until a new studio was completed behind the Rockwells' new home.

Technology

During Norman Rockwell's lifetime, technology made major advances and he documented Americans' enthusiasm for their new machines. Communications technology, in particular, developed rapidly during this period, removing the barrier of distance and allowing Americans to talk with one another and eventually to see each other.

A U.S. Army poster that Rockwell painted during the First World War shows a telegraph operator sending Morse code. In 1919 a Rockwell *Post* cover featured a woman using her telephone party line to eavesdrop on her neighbors.

Eventually wires would no longer be needed to transmit messages. By 1920 amateurs could transmit and receive coded messages through the wireless, as Rockwell depicted in his painting of a grandfather listening in to his grandson's Morse code transmission, featured on the February 21, 1920, cover of *The Literary Digest*.

Radios were the all the rage in the early 1920s. The first commercial radio station broadcasted the results of the Harding-Cox presidential election of November 1920. The sale of receiving sets and component parts for home radios grew rapidly, and by 1922 there were 564 licensed broadcasting stations in the United States. A

LEFT, TOP:
Grandpa Listening In on the Wireless
Oil on canvas
22 × 19.5 inches (56 × 49.5cm)
First published on the cover of *The Literary Digest*, February 21, 1920

LEFT, BOTTOM:
Old Couple Listening to Radio
First published on the cover of *The Saturday Evening Post*, May 20, 1922

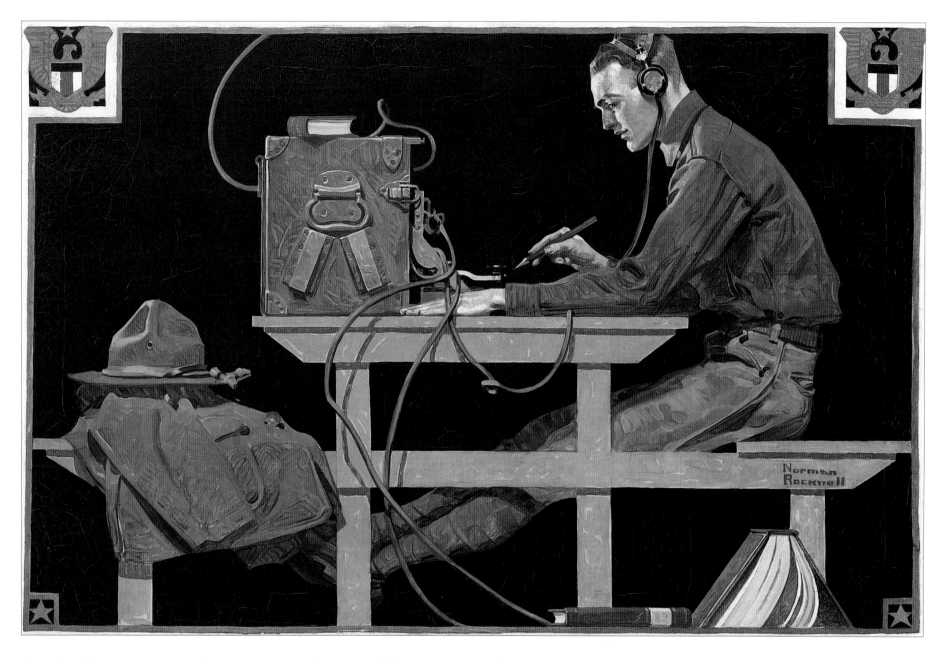

Saturday Evening Post cover from May 1922 shows an old man enjoying the opera through his headset while his wife strains to catch some of the melody.

Electric light was an innovation promoted during the 1920s. Rockwell's advertising campaign for Edson Mazda Lampworks featured at least twenty full-color oil paintings. The theme of the campaign was that life was more pleasant with the use of electric light. The company was promoting electricity over gas. To reflect this, the paintings showed how a flick of an electric switch could illuminate an entire room or the music score on a piano. The paintings depicted families reading, relaxing, and enjoying each other's company in well-lit surroundings. He also painted what life was like before electricity, showing women

The U.S. Army Teaches Trades
   (*also* The Telegrapher)
Oil on canvas
19.5 × 29.5 inches (49.5 × 75cm)
First used as a recruiting poster for the U.S. Army, 1919

dipping candles and preparing lamp wicks and an old man unable to see an intruder because the kerosene lamp's glow is too feeble.

Moving pictures and movie theaters grew in popularity during this period. Rockwell understood America's fascination with Hollywood because it was a passion he shared. He did an advertisement for Paramount Pictures in 1921 that shows a family buying movie tickets. In 1930, while in Hollywood himself, he painted a young Mary Pickford look-alike sitting on a bench outside a closed casting office. Beside her sit two older actors also waiting for their turn to become stars. He painted Gary Cooper as a cowboy in buckskin having lipstick applied to his mouth before going on the set. Rockwell also painted young fans in their bedrooms, looking with dreamy eyes into their Hollywood sweethearts' photographs. He showed the flip side of America's love affair with the movies, in a painting of two out-of-work members of the Gaiety Dance Team; vaudeville was dead and such acts, which had once traveled across the country, had lost their audiences to the movie projector.

Another technological phenomenon captured by Rockwell's paintbrush was the arrival of television. In 1931 television technology was available, but the military establishment restricted the manufacture of receivers during the Second World War. With the end of the war the television broadcasting industry experienced rapid growth. One million receivers were in use by 1949, and just nine years later that figure had risen to fifty million. Rockwell captured Americans' delight with the new technology in a Post cover from November 1949. It shows an antenna being installed on a roof and the owner's happy amazement when it actually picks up images from the sky. Rockwell drew two television advertisements for Dumont in the early 1950s, which show watching television as a family affair. In a third Dumont advertisement Rockwell painted two children abandoning their toys for the enchanted land of television.

Two Girls Looking at Movie Star's Photo
Oil on canvas
32 × 26 inches (81 × 66cm)
First published on the cover of *The Saturday Evening Post*,
  February 19, 1938

Gaiety Dance Team
Oil on canvas
36 × 29 inches (91.5 × 73.5cm)
First published on the cover of
    The Saturday Evening Post,
    June 12, 1937

Movie Starlet and Reporters
First published on the cover of
The Saturday Evening Post,
March 7, 1936

America Takes Flight

In December 1903, Orville Wright flew a biplane 120 feet (37m) in twelve seconds to become the first man to fly in an airplane. Nineteen years later, in 1922, Norman Rockwell himself took flight.

I remember the first time I went up in an airplane. I was judging a beauty contest in Atlantic City. The airplanes were very new. This was a hydroplane and they offered us judges a free ride. Another illustrator, Dean Cornwall, and myself went over to its hangar—a very amateurish thing. This was a monoplane. The motor was up and back of the wings. Before we went up we had to sign a piece of paper, which you don't have to do anymore, saying that the airplane company was not responsible for anything that you suffered while you were up in the plane....We put on our helmets because there was no cabin to the plane. You just sat out in the open air. We took off and went up. In as much as we were free passengers, the pilot was going to have some fun with us. He didn't do a loop-the-loop but he did some beautiful nose-dives. All this was in a heavy old aquaplane which had these big pontoons under it. We were very thrilled with it. There was a terrible racket because the motor was right behind us with the big ol' propeller going.

We came down all right and after we got down the same pilot took up another passenger who happened to be a skywriter. This fellow, I think, was working for the Lucky Strike Company. He'd go up in an airplane, not a hydroplane, and make the name Lucky Strike in the sky. We had no more gotten out and were taking off our helmets when they took off. Evidently, they said afterwards that the pilot must have let the Lucky Strike pilot take over the controls. The Lucky Strike pilot wasn't used to the hydroplane with the weight of the pontoons...and he must have tried to sideslip or turn the plane too fast or something. The two of them crashed. It was a horrible accident. Dean Cornwall and I were standing there and we saw the whole thing. The engine, as I said, was behind the people who sat in the plane. When they went into the sandbar the engine carried them down so many feet into the sand. Everyone was yelling and everything.

Uncle Sam Flying
Oil on canvas
34 × 24 inches (86 × 61cm)
First published on the cover of *The Saturday Evening Post*,
January 21, 1928

Pioneer of the Air
  (*also* Portrait of Charles Lindbergh)
  Oil on canvas
  22.5 × 18.5 inches (57 × 47cm)
  First published on the cover of
    The Saturday Evening Post,
    July 23, 1927

Dean Cornwall and I got into a row boat. One of the men at the hangar said, "Will you take this lady? This is the widow of the pilot." So we rowed her out. The poor woman was in hysterics. We were out there an hour or so. They had to dig them out and hoist the engine off and what was left was these poor fellows way down in the sand.

In 1927, Charles Lindbergh was the first to fly nonstop across the Atlantic. Rockwell captured the heroism of this early air pioneer for *The Saturday Evening Post.* He completed the cover in twenty-six hours so that it would still be timely when published.

During the summer of 1927, Rockwell and his friends had a hair-raising flight on a French airplane crossing the English Channel from Britain to France. While the four passengers were bounced around in their seats by the turbulence, the copilot spent the trip sitting on the floor with his back to the pilot, reading a paperback. The passengers resorted to swigs of scotch to calm their nerves. The plane rattled and clanked, its wooden floorboards rising up and down when it finally landed at Le Bourget's airfield. Surprisingly, a Rockwell *Post* cover from six months later shows a serene Uncle Sam flying among the clouds (page 49).

Flying eventually became safer and better regulated. By 1938 it was considered so safe, in fact, that Rockwell painted an old woman flying as a passenger in an enclosed cabin. In this *Post* cover the passenger appears to be very comfortable as she sits with a map of her air voyage spread out on her lap and peers out the window with excited interest.

Rockwell flew around the world doing sketches for Pan American Airlines in 1956. He sketched the people and sights of Paris, Barcelona, Rome, Istanbul, Beirut, Karachi, Calcutta, Benares, Rangoon, Bangkok, Hong Kong, Tokyo, and Hawaii. These were very different experiences from his initial flight of 1922.

The Two World Wars

Throughout his long and prolific career, Norman Rockwell painted images that Americans could relate to and dealt with issues that concerned the public at large. When America went to war, Rockwell painted war experiences, but he painted very little fighting. Of the more than sixty war-related paintings he did during the First and Second World Wars, only one depicts a combat scene. He never went overseas as a war correspondent. Instead, Rockwell stayed in the United States and painted what he was familiar with. He chose subjects he felt confident painting.

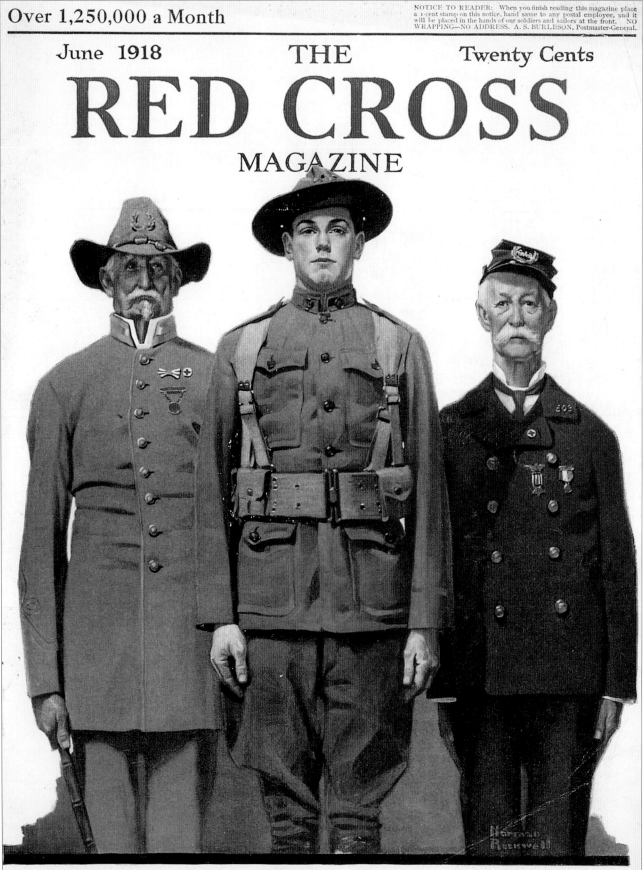

Veterans of Two Wars
Oil on canvas
27 × 22 inches (68.5 × 56cm)
First published on the cover of
    The Red Cross Magazine, June 1918

FAR LEFT:
Mess Cooks
First published in *Afloat and Ashore*, November 13, 1918

LEFT:
All For One—One For All
First published in *Afloat and Ashore*, November 13, 1918

When the United States entered World War I, Rockwell was a young man of twenty-three years. Up until 1917 he had painted children for *The Saturday Evening Post* covers and did illustrations for many different children's magazines. Once the United States joined the war effort Rockwell continued to paint children. He painted a healthy, smiling little French girl washing an American soldier's ears and another trying to communicate with a soldier. In yet another depiction, an American in uniform tries to teach a young European how to play baseball. The children are picturesque in their wooden shoes and European dress, though they are not an accurate reflection of what life was like overseas.

Rockwell painted happy images of wartime. He painted a group of soldiers singing their hearts out to the music of a banjo and two soldiers in a comfortable-looking trench playing cards by candlelight. He was not painting trench warfare—he just dressed his models in First World War uniforms.

During the First World War, I had done pictures of the doughboys in France, but it had all been fakery. I'd taken familiar scenes—a little girl pinning a flower in a soldier's buttonhole, a mother mending her son's socks—and altered them to fit the new locale by dressing the models in costume—soldiers' uniforms, Dutch caps, wooden shoes. It hadn't seemed to matter that the pictures lacked authenticity. I had been young then and unsophisticated, just trying to get ahead, establish myself as an illustrator.

LEFT, TOP:
Are We Downhearted?
(*also* Group of Smiling Soldiers' Faces)
Oil on canvas
20 × 20 inches (51 × 51cm)
First published on the cover of *Life*,
November 28, 1918

LEFT, BOTTOM:
A Tribute from France
(*also* Soldier and Little French Girl)
Oil on canvas
26 × 23 inches (66 × 58.5cm)
First published on the cover of *Judge*,
August 10, 1918

During wartime, ideas for covers came easily. Newspapers in 1917 reported that the French had welcomed the Americans, or doughboys, with great enthusiasm. This prompted Rockwell to paint a little French girl putting a flower in an American soldier's buttonhole. On and off military bases people would yell, "Are we downhearted?" and the expected response was a resounding "NO!" Rockwell reflected this cheer of the day by filling a canvas with smiling military faces and titling it "Are We Downhearted?"

Not all Rockwell's World War I paintings featured smiling faces. He captured the anxiety of many Americans in the 1918 *Life* cover "Till the Boys Come Home," which he was inspired to paint when one of his child models mentioned that his sister's boyfriend had left for the war. The painting depicts four young women waiting on a hillside under a forbidding sky. Beside them on the hill is a letter from a loved one stamped "censor" and an unfinished pair of socks one of them is knitting to send overseas. Below the hill, part of a larger crowd can be seen anxiously looking east across the Atlantic. Rockwell captured the horror of war in the angry eyes of a disabled veteran for a *Literary Digest* cover entitled "Story of the Lost Battalion" (page 56). The veteran is shown recounting his story to a sailor and a young boy, the veteran's cane resting at his side.

Norman Rockwell was personally committed to serving his country during the First World War. When the initial draft call was made the military exempted him from service, but he did help the authorities during night patrols of the New Rochelle harbor. Eventually the sight of wounded merchant seamen prompted him to try to get the enlistment officers to change their minds and let him join. The doctors rejected his request because he was seventeen pounds (8kg) underweight for his height. He persisted by going to another enlistment center, where Rockwell recognized the petty officer at the scales as being a fellow student from the Art Students League. The former student convinced the doctors to allow Rockwell to take the "treatment" and bulk up his weight with bananas, doughnuts, and water in order to barely meet the regulations. Rockwell was as-

Till the Boys Come Home
(*also* Women Sitting by
Edge of Sea)
Oil on canvas
30 × 42 inches (76 × 107cm)
First published on the cover of
Life, August 15, 1918

Story of the Lost Battalion
   (*also* Soldier Telling War Story)
Oil on canvas
25.5 × 23.5 inches (65 × 60cm)
First published on the cover of
   The Literary Digest, March 1, 1919

signed to the Naval Reserve Base in Charleston, South Carolina, where he was made art editor of the base's publication, *Afloat and Ashore.* Two days a week he drew cartoons and did layout for the newspaper; the rest of the week he was permitted to do his own work as long as it was somehow related to the U.S. Navy. He continued to do magazine covers and painted portraits of his fellow seamen, their officers, and eventually portraits of Commander Mark St. Clair Ellis and his wife. After four months in the service, Rockwell left the navy and returned to civilian life.

Rockwell painted thirty-three war-related covers during the two years that Americans fought in the First World War. His war paintings were featured on the covers of *Judge, Leslie's, The Literary Digest, The Recruiters' Bulletin, The Red Cross Magazine,* and *The Saturday Evening Post.* While many of the covers are full paintings that fill the page with detail, his *Post* covers from this period mainly feature figures in the foreground with a white background.

Rockwell's first *Post* cover from the Second World War period was painted before the United States actually joined the Allies overseas. He wanted to depict the experiences of a young civilian drafted to serve his country. In 1941 Rockwell chose a young man he met at a square dance in West Arlington to be the model for Willie Gillis, who was to become one of Rockwell's most popular characters.

His name was Bob Buck and he was, luckily, exempt from the draft. I painted him in situations which I thought were typical of an average draftee's life in the army: receiving a food package from home, sleeping late during a furlough, peeling potatoes. The series became quite popular and I figured I was set for the duration.

Then, gosh darn it, Bob Buck somehow or other managed to get himself into the navy. So I sorrowfully laid Willie to rest.

No! said the editors of the Post. *You can't drop him; he's too popular. Which posed a problem. I didn't have a model. All I had were old photographs of Bob Buck. I painted Willie's girl faithfully sleeping at midnight on New Year's Eve, three photographs of Willie tacked on the wall above her bed.*

And then I had a really bright idea. I did Willie and his warlike ancestors, portraits of the Gillis men in uniform from great-great-great-grandfather Gillis in his Revolutionary War uniform down through great-great-grandfather Gillis (War of 1812), great-grandfather Gillis (Civil War), grandfather Gillis

Portrait of Commander Mark St. Clair Ellis
Oil on canvas
20 × 14.75 inches (51 × 37.5cm)

Willie Gillis: Food Package
First published on the cover of
The Saturday Evening Post,
October 4, 1941

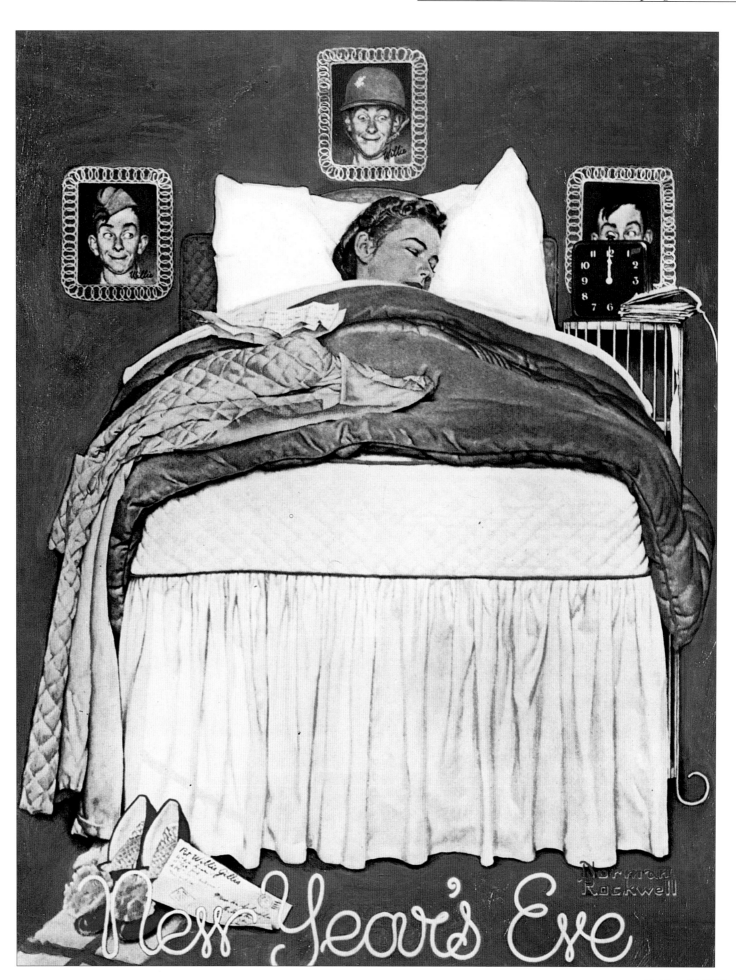

Willie Gillis: New Year's Eve
First published on the cover of
The Saturday Evening Post,
January 1, 1944

THE SATURDAY EVENING

POST

JUNE 27, 1942
VOLUME 214 NUMBER 52

10¢

WHAT
TO DO
IN A
BLACKOUT

property of
Willie Gillis,
Jr.

Norman
Rockwell

THE CASE FOR THE MINORITIES
WENDELL L. WILLKIE

OUR TWO MONTHS ON CORREGIDOR CABOT COVILLE

LEFT:
**Willie Gillis: What To Do in
a Blackout**
First published on the cover of
The Saturday Evening Post,
June 27, 1942

OPPOSITE:
Willie Gillis
Oil on board
13.25 × 10.625 inches (34 × 27cm)
First published on the cover of
The Saturday Evening Post,
September 16, 1944

Willie Gillis in College
Oil on canvas
36 × 35 inches (91.5 × 90cm)
First published on the cover of *The Saturday Evening Post,*
  October 5, 1946

(Spanish-American War), Willie's father (World War I) to Willie himself, grinning innocently from under his khaki kettle of a helmet. The six portraits were all painted from the same photograph of Bob Buck, but I altered the expressions somewhat, crowned each Gillis with a different hairdo, made the portraits different shapes and sizes, put them in a variety of frames, hung them on a flowered wallpaper and, presto-whiz-bang, I had a Post *cover.*

During the Second World War the *Post* changed its look. In 1942 Ben Hibbs took over as its new editor and re-designed the magazine's cover. The word "Post" was blown up to dominate the top left corner. Rockwell was using photographs to compose his covers, a technique that enabled him to use many different models in a variety of different positions. Consequently, the backgrounds of the cover illustrations became more detailed and complex.

The one painting Rockwell did of actual fighting is a U.S. Army poster from World War II that shows a machine gunner—his uniform peeling off his back—shooting his last round. It cries out, "Let's give him Enough and On Time." The poster was painted for the U.S. Army Ordnance Department and was issued in 1942, when the entire nation was gearing up for massive increases in production.

Rockwell's Second World War paintings focus mainly on civilian life. Rockwell painted a coal miner for a government poster. Pinned to the miner are two stars that represent two family members serving overseas. On the cover of *The Saturday Evening Post,* Rosie the Riveter proudly munches on her lunch, fully

Let's give him Enough and On Time
Oil on canvas
42 × 50 inches (106.5 × 127cm)
First used as a war poster for the U.S. Army, 1942

aware of the contribution women are making to the war effort in the factories across the United States (page 65). On another *Post* cover the Liberty Girl struggles across the page, lugging all the responsibilities she's had to take on to keep the country running (page 64). Rockwell painted a man, too old to enlist, attentively listening to his radio and charting the war maneuvers on his maps from his armchair (page 67). One war painting the *Post* didn't publish shows a group of men in a neighborhood diner listening to the radio (page 67). They are waiting for news of the D-Day invasion. Like Rockwell, their war experience was based on the home front.

When America entered the conflict, Rockwell was forty-seven. Too old to enlist, he still wanted to make a personal contribution to the war effort. He and

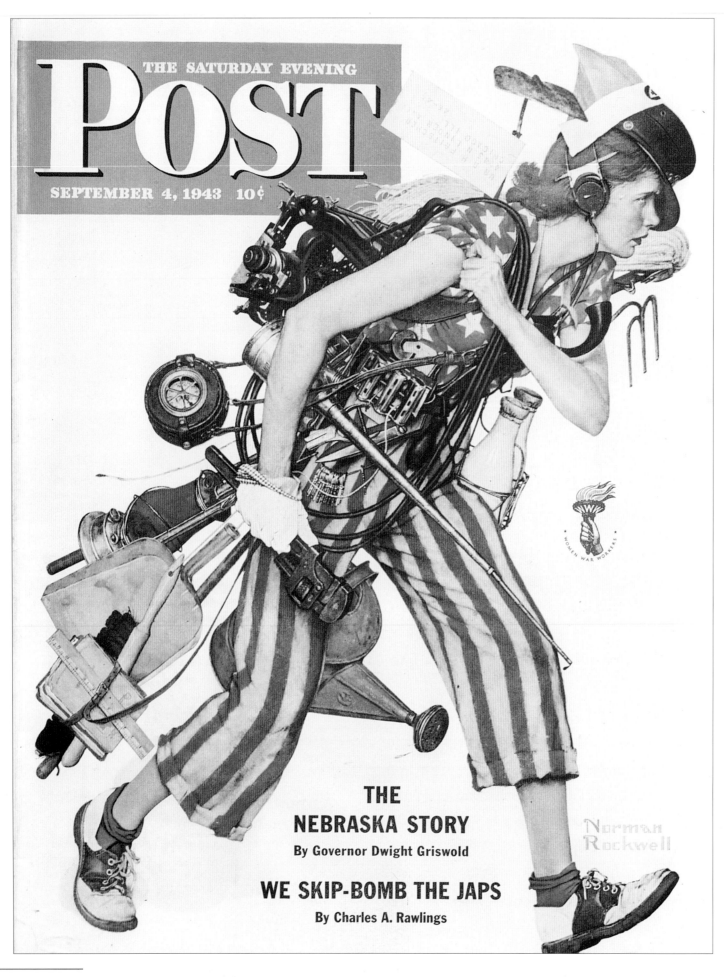

LEFT:
Liberty Girl
First published on the cover of
The Saturday Evening Post,
September 4, 1943

OPPOSITE:
Rosie the Riveter
First published on the cover of
The Saturday Evening Post,
May 29, 1943

ABOVE, LEFT:

Mine America's Coal

(*also* Portrait of a Coal Miner)

Oil on canvas

21 × 14 inches (53.5 × 35.5cm)

First used as a war poster for the U.S. Office of War
Information, 1943

ABOVE, RIGHT:

Disabled Veteran

Oil on canvas

43 × 34 inches (109 × 86.5cm)

First published in *The Saturday Evening Post,* July 1944

fellow illustrator Mead Schaeffer did some sketches and took their ideas to Washington. Like the enlistment officers Rockwell encountered in World War I, the Washington officials initially rejected Rockwell's offer. When he showed his color sketches to the officials at the Office of War Information he was told that "[during] the last war you illustrators did the posters. This war we're going to use fine arts men, real artists. If you want to make a contribution to the war effort you can do some of these pen and ink drawings for the marine corps' calisthenics manual."

On his return from Washington, Rockwell stopped in Philadelphia and showed his sketches to the *Post*'s Ben Hibbs, who recognized their potential. Rockwell had visually represented President Franklin D. Roosevelt's statement of what was at stake during the Second World War in a series known as the Four Freedoms.

Rockwell had seen Roosevelt's ideas come to life in rural Vermont. In Arlington he had attended a town meeting where a local farmer had stood up to speak against something that everyone else in town supported. The people of the town let him speak. Rockwell realized that he could illustrate the abstract liberties Roosevelt had enumerated through simple, everyday scenes. The New England town meeting would represent "Freedom of Speech" (page 68); "Freedom from Want" would be a Thanksgiving dinner (page 69); "Freedom from Fear" would be parents tucking their children in to bed at night while the newspaper headline told of the bombings and death of a far-off war (page 70); and "Freedom to Worship" was initially portrayed using a group of men from different religions waiting and good-naturedly gossiping in a barbershop. Later, the painting "Freedom to Worship" was reworked to show many different heads representing different religions bowed in prayer and contemplation. Across the

BELOW, LEFT:
War News
(*also* Listening for the Invasion of D–Day)
Oil on canvas
41.25 × 40.5 inches (105 × 103cm)
Intended for *The Saturday Evening Post*, c. 1945

BELOW, RIGHT:
Man Charting War Maneuvers
Oil on canvas
35 × 33 inches (89 × 84cm)
First published on the cover of *The Saturday Evening Post*,
April 29, 1944

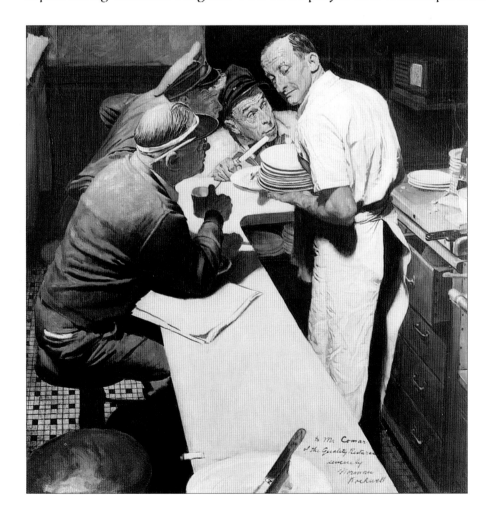

Freedom of Speech
Oil on canvas
45.75 × 35.5 inches (116 × 90cm)
First published in *The Saturday Evening Post*, February 20, 1943

Freedom from Want
Oil on canvas
45.75 × 35.5 inches
  (116 × 90cm)
First published in *The
  Saturday Evening Post,*
  March 6, 1943

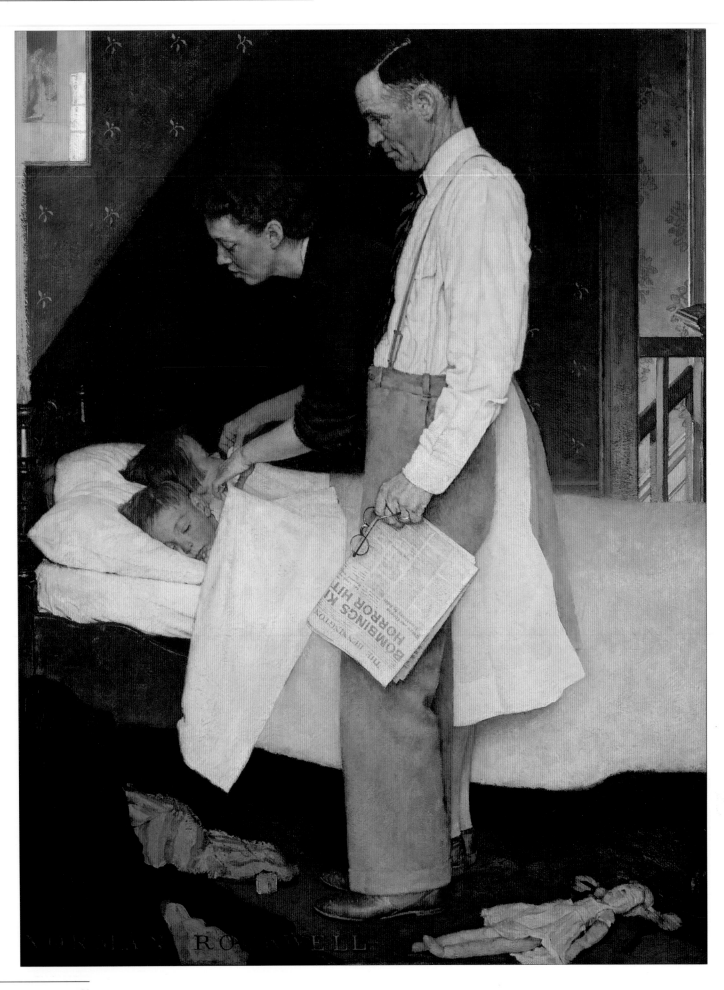

Freedom from Fear
Oil on canvas
45.75 × 35.5 inches (116 × 90cm)
First published in *The Saturday
Evening Post*, March 13, 1943

Freedom to Worship
Oil on canvas
46 × 35.5 inches (117 × 90cm)
First published in *The Saturday Evening Post*, February 1943

RIGHT:

The Homecoming

Oil on canvas

28 × 22 inches (71 × 56cm)

First published on the cover of
The Saturday Evening Post,
May 26, 1945

OPPOSITE:

Homecoming Marine

Oil on canvas

46 × 42 inches (117 × 106.5cm)

First published on the cover of
The Saturday Evening Post,
October 13, 1945

ABOVE:
Home on Leave
(*also* Sailor in Hammock)
First published on the cover of *The Saturday Evening Post,*
September 15, 1945

OPPOSITE:
Income Tax
First published on the cover of *The Saturday Evening Post,*
March 17, 1945

top of the painting is inscribed, "Each according to the dictates of his own conscience" (page 71).

Hibbs published the Four Freedoms as inside features in the Post and accompanied each painting with an essay on the subject. The paintings were highly acclaimed from the moment they were published. The Post printed reproductions, the Office of War Information printed 2.5 million posters made from the paintings, and the originals went on tour in a special campaign to sell war bonds. At the end of the campaign more than 1.2 million people across the United States had seen the traveling show and more than $132,992,539 in war bonds had been sold.

When the war finally ended and the soldiers came home, Rockwell captured the poignant relief of a nation. One painting shows a whole neighborhood rejoicing as a soldier returns to his mother's open arms in a tenement in Troy, New York (page 72). Respect and admiration for a young marine are clearly evident in a painting of a Vermont garage where friends gather to hear the hero tell his stories from the war in the Pacific (page 73). And there's no mistaking the profound love and gratitude in a mother's glance in another painting as she peels the Thanksgiving potatoes with her boy, now a man, safely back at her side (page 77).

Rockwell's depiction of the civilian war experience managed to tap into emotions shared by the American public. His Four Freedoms helped to rally support for the war effort, and his covers reflected the nation's concern during the war and the great relief when the fighting was over. His First World War paintings were painted by a young enthusiastic artist too inexperienced to be able to adequately portray the deep emotion of wartime. By the Second World War he had matured as a man and as an artist. His maturity and vast talent enabled him to capture on canvas what many Americans were feeling in their souls.

THE SATURDAY EVENING

POST

JULY 6, 1946   10¢

BEGINNING: **Double Treasure**

By CLARENCE BUDINGTON KELLAND

The Book-of-the-Month Club

By PETE MARTIN

LEFT:
Statue of Liberty
Oil on canvas
24 × 14 inches (61 × 35.5cm)
First published on the cover of
    The Saturday Evening Post,
    July 6, 1946

OPPOSITE:
Thanksgiving: Mother and Son Peeling Potatoes
Oil on canvas
35 × 33.5 inches (89 × 85cm)
First published on the cover of
    The Saturday Evening Post,
    November 24, 1945

Thanksgiving

norman rockwell

CHAPTER THREE

Commercial Artist, Reporter, Illustrator?

1945–1959

Norman Rockwell continued to paint in the studio he had built behind his West Arlington home in Vermont. He painted every day, seven days a week, from eight o'clock in the morning until five o'clock in the evening. He took half a day off for Thanksgiving and, because his wife, Mary, insisted, a whole day off for Christmas. The family did take occasional trips to New York City, and in 1945 they traveled to California. They returned to California in 1948 to stay for a year, and Rockwell rented a studio at the Los Angeles County Art Institute. In 1952 Rockwell painted a portrait of General Dwight D. Eisenhower for the *Post* that was the first in a series of portraits he did of presidential candidates. Two years later President Eisenhower invited Rockwell to the White House for a private dinner party. In 1953 the Rockwell family moved to Stockbridge, Massachusetts. Rockwell always said that one should keep moving in order to not be left behind; indeed, he feared being "stuck in the mud" or becoming "old hat" if he didn't change locations at least once every twenty years. The Rockwells chose to make their home in Stockbridge, where Mary could get the treatment she needed (for depression) at the Austin Riggs Center,

OPPOSITE:
Portrait of Dwight D. Eisenhower
First published on the cover of *The Saturday Evening Post*, October 11, 1952

a psychiatric institution. In 1956 Rockwell flew around the world on a "clipper ship tour" making sketches for a Pan American Airlines' advertising campaign. He painted another portrait of President Eisenhower in 1956 in addition to a painting of the presidential candidate Adlai E. Stevenson. In August 1959 Mary died unexpectedly. She and Norman had been married for twenty-nine years.

Commercial Art

When Rockwell attended art school he had no intention of becoming a commercial artist and swore he'd never accept a commission to paint advertisements.

> *Art Young, Charley Kuntz, and I signed our names in blood, swearing never to prostitute our art, never to do advertising jobs, never to make more than fifty dollars a week. That sounds like something only fine-arts students would do, but all three of us were dead-set on being illustrators. (That oath has long since been broken. But it signifies nothing. At the time I was like the little boy who vowed he would never grow up to be a man—I just didn't know myself.)*

It didn't take Rockwell long to change his mind. In fact, he began accepting commissions to do advertisements soon after he left art school. While at times throughout his career he felt uncomfortable accepting commercial commissions, the combined effect of his enormous drive to paint, his desire to please his public, and the need to support his family meant that by the end of his career he had accepted commercial commissions from more than 150 companies. He produced paintings and drawings for Hallmark Christmas cards, Boy Scouts calendars, Brown and Bigelow calendars, and numerous advertisers.

Given Rockwell's early success as an illustrator for children's magazines, advertisers wanted the young artist to paint children with their products. In 1912 Rockwell sketched a Heinz Baked Beans advertisement showing two Boy Scouts cooking their can of beans over an open fire. The Fisk Rubber Company used

ABOVE:
What a Difference Light Makes!
(*also* Young Couple Surprised by Young Brother)
First used as an advertisement for Edison Mazda Lamps, 1920

OPPOSITE:
Orange Crush
Oil on canvas
First used as an advertisement for Orange Crush, 1921

Rockwell's illustrations of young boys and their bicycles to sell bicycle tires and to encourage boys to join a Fisk Bicycle Club. During the First World War, club members were said to be "doing their bit" by making themselves useful. Fisk Club members may not be old enough to be at the front, said the ad, but "their labors in bicycle patrols, delivering messages, as Red Cross assistants and so on are an excellent training in discipline and character-building that develops manly and honorable men." Rockwell's tramps, small boys, and dogs were also used to sell Fisk automobile tires in the early 1920s.

Like the Mazda Edison promotional campaign celebrating electric light, Rockwell's advertisements for Perfection Oil Heaters suggest that home life in 1917 could be enhanced. The kerosene space heaters were promoted as a necessity for people trying to keep their loved ones warm when houses were said to be drafty, coal expensive, and natural gas scarce. In one of the paintings, a woman prepares for her husband's return by arranging the heater, his slippers, and his house coat beside his comfortable chair where his book and pipe already wait for him. In 1918 people were encouraged to buy the portable space heater for patriotic reasons—to "save the nation's coal."

Rockwell's advertisements from this early period until the 1930s are similar in style to his covers. They were frequently painted in oil and told a story not always connected to the product. The ads from these early years featured boys in short pants and triple-knee stockings, dogs, vagabonds, and grandfathers in a variety of nostalgic scenes.

In the early 1930s Coca-Cola used Rockwell's paintings of country boys with fishing poles and lovable dogs to advertise the "pause that refreshes." These ads were some of the few Rockwell did during the 1930s and 1940s. Writing to her parents in California from Paris in 1932, Mary Rockwell identified her husband's internal struggle between commercial art and what she called "artistic art."

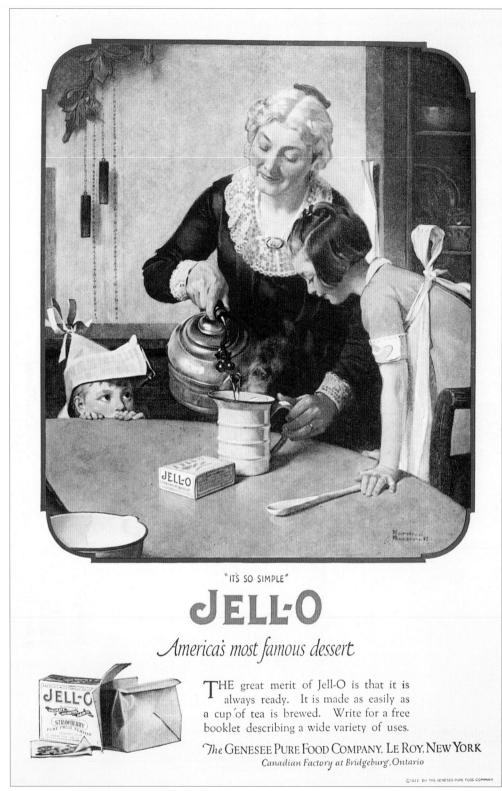

"It's So Simple"
First used as an advertisement for
Genesee Pure Food Company, 1923

Father's Easy Chair
First used as an advertisement for
Perfection Oil Heaters, 1917

Truly, this trip is the best thing that ever happened to us. It has made Norman a different person. He has found the courage to do what he wants for six months which shows that after two years of struggling—and it truly was that—he has at last come out in the open and knows what he wants to do, which is experiment with all sorts of things for the next six months to become an artistic artist instead of a commercial one. Don't fear that he will go modern. That is his last thought. Never. For a while that worried him; but as I told you the Louvre inspires him and modern galleries do not, so now he's decided to be the thing that is in him to be—to do what he did, only in a finer way.

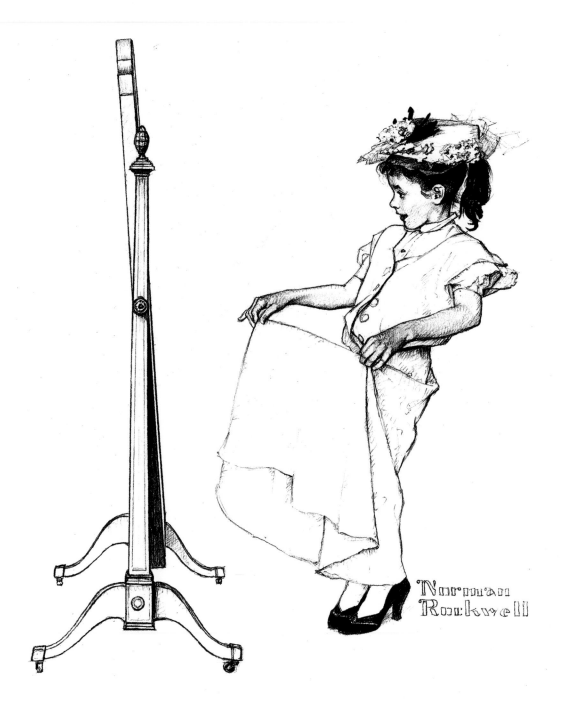

Girl in Front of Mirror
Pencil on paper
14 × 12 inches (35.5 × 30.5cm)
First used as an advertisement for Massachusetts Mutual, 1955

As Mary's letters show, Rockwell was trying to distance himself from commercial art. In 1935 the artist was commissioned to illustrate Mark Twain's *The Adventures of Tom Sawyer* and *The Adventures of Huckleberry Finn*. He accepted the job with great enthusiasm for it was "pure" illustration.

During the 1950s Rockwell again accepted numerous advertising commissions. No longer restricting himself to oil paintings, he used line drawings for many advertisements from this period. Campaigns for Fidelity Bank, Swift baby foods, Texas Commerce Bank, and, most notably, the Massachusetts Mutual Life Insurance Company featured happy family members engaged in a variety of different activities. Rockwell did eighty-one drawings for the Massachusetts Mutual series, which featured the joys and responsibilities of American family life. The postwar baby boom was in full swing, and Rockwell documented the American focus on the family with endearing scenes of domesticity. He featured children's portraits in advertisements for Crest toothpaste and for Kellogg's corn flakes. A Ford commission for a farming tractor calendar shows a community supper where the men are serving the dinner. Given the delight and hilarity around the dinner table, this role reversal appears to have been a rare event.

In 1968 Rockwell used oil paintings to depict fourteen different workers occupied in various aspects of the steel industry for a commission from the Sharon Steel Corporation. These paintings show highly trained workers going about their responsibilities with great skill and professionalism. Top Value Stamps catalog covers were also done in oil but featured light and often humorous family scenes from the early 1970s. The Top Value Stamps paintings are reminiscent of earlier Rockwell cover illustrations. They feature boys with their dogs, girls with mirrors, and a teenage couple coming in late from a date.

An advertisement for ATO construction scaffolding shows how perplexing the changing times could be. Two construction workers, their lunch pails open, gaze in disbelief at the barefoot hippie who sits strumming his guitar and singing on the adjoining scaffolding. The ad is called "You've Got to Be Kidding."

Rockwell painted fifty calendars for the Boy Scouts between 1924 and 1976 and also produced paintings for Brown and Bigelow calendars, which mainly featured scenes of children and older people. Just as he had ambiguous feelings about advertising, Rockwell wasn't always very enthusiastic when it was time to start work on his yearly painting for the Boy Scouts. There was little room for Rockwell's humorous stories in these paintings, the point of view being dictated by the client. For instance, the Boy Scouts insisted that their badges be correctly positioned on the uniform, and sent paintings back to Rockwell if he placed the badges improperly or didn't get the color right. There was to be no ambivalence in a scouting painting, and Rockwell found the unquestioning scout difficult to portray. Even when Rockwell painted religious themes his message was usually one of tolerance, and he frequently softened the lofty overtones with a leavening of humor. In a painting for the Boy Scouts he was forced to show pure and resolute dedication without any frayed edges, and this made him uncomfortable.

The number of commercial commissions Rockwell would accept varied over the years, and although he produced hundreds of advertisements he was always ambivalent toward commercial art. In spite of his early and sustained success, Norman Rockwell was modest and insecure about his work. Over the years, he struggled to find a label to describe what he did (he wasn't secure enough with his talent to call himself a fine artist). He also knew at one level that he was a commercial artist but found the term a bit raw. He settled the issue by referring to himself as an illustrator and he titled his autobiography *My Adventures as an Illustrator.*

Bus Stop
Pencil on paper
19 × 10.75 inches (48 × 27.5cm)
First used as an advertisement for Massachusetts Mutual, 1956

BELOW:
Mother's Birthday
Pencil on paper
14.25 × 18 inches (36 × 45.5cm)
First used as an advertisement for
Massachusetts Mutual, 1963

RIGHT:
Doll Lullaby
Pencil on paper
13 × 13.5 inches (33 × 34.5cm)
First used as an advertisement for
Massachusetts Mutual, 1960

Norman Rockwell in Voting Booth
Pencil on paper
13.25 × 10.25 inches (33.5 × 26cm)
First used as an advertisement for Massachusetts Mutual, 1960

Family Picnic
Pencil on paper
16 × 17 inches (40.5 × 43cm)
First used as an advertisement for
   Massachusetts Mutual, 1962

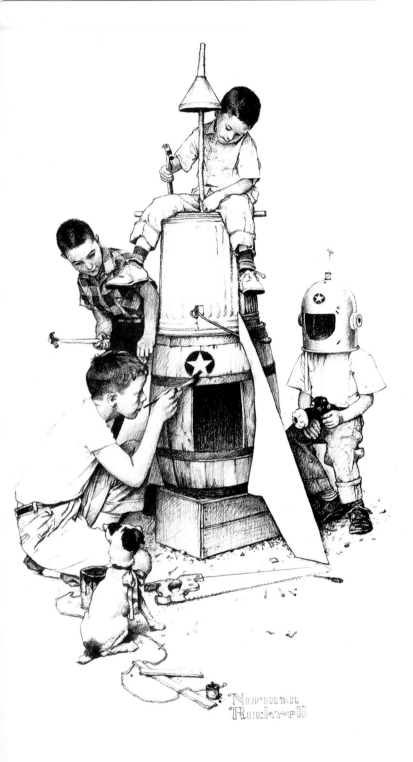

Space Ship
Pencil on paper
21 × 13 inches (53.5 × 33cm)
First used as an advertisement for
Massachusetts Mutual, 1959–1960

RIGHT:
Football Hero
12.375 × 11 inches (31.5 × 28cm)
First used as an advertisement for
Massachusetts Mutual, 1961

BELOW:

Boy at Mirror

Pencil on paper

15.75 × 12.25 inches (40 × 31cm)

First used as an advertisement for
Massachusetts Mutual, 1959

RIGHT:

Father Leads His Son
Through His Plant

Pencil on paper

13.5 × 13.5 inches (34 × 34cm)

First used as an advertisement
for Texas Commerce Bank,
1955

BELOW:

For Dad's Approval

Pencil on paper

14 × 20 inches (35.5 × 51cm)

First used as an advertisement
for Massachusetts Mutual,
1950s

LEFT:

Baby's First Step

Pencil on paper

12.625 × 15.375 inches (32 × 39cm)

First used as an advertisement for
Massachusetts Mutual, 1958

LEFT:
The American Way
(*also* Soldier Feeding Girl)
Oil
29 × 23 inches (73.5 × 58.5cm)
First used as an advertisement for
Disabled American Veterans, 1944

OPPOSITE:
The Lineman
(*also* Telephone Lineman on Pole)
Oil on canvas
57 × 42.125 inches (144.5 × 107cm)
First used as an advertisement for
AT&T, 1949

Art as Reportage

Throughout his long career Rockwell adapted his work to different situations and different magazine styles. During the Second World War he began to use his art as a form of reportage.

Rockwell's work on the Four Freedoms and his promotion of war bonds involved him intimately in the Second World War effort. In 1943 he used his drawings to report on the war experience when he and fellow illustrator Mead Schaeffer visited a paratrooper's training base. Rockwell sketched the troops leaving for their port of embarkation to England. The group of sketches he did of his visit was entitled "A Night on a Troop Train" and shows the paratroopers lounging in the train, gazing out the window at a passing town, and trying to get some sleep. The men are lined up on the station's platform and are shown being admired by a small boy. Rockwell even put himself in a sketch of the soldiers shaving. Not long after these troops left for England they were dropped behind the German lines in France, on D-Day.

RIGHT:
A Night on a Troop Train
"Penny Ante."
First published in *The Saturday Evening Post,* May 8, 1943

ABOVE:
A Night on a Troop Train
"He's passing his hometown."
First published in *The Saturday Evening Post,* May 8, 1943

RIGHT:
A Night on a Troop Train
"2 A.M."
First published in *The Saturday Evening Post,* May 8, 1943

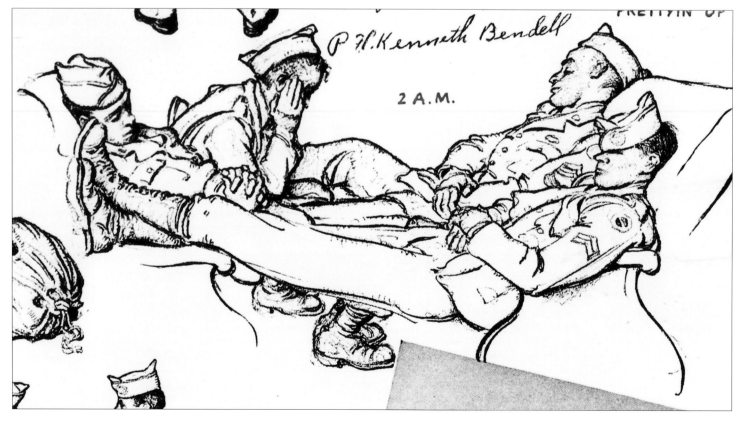

When Rockwell's studio burned down in May 1943 he used sketches to tell the tale of the fire. This time the small charcoal sketches of the firemen, the fire, and the Rockwell family were drawn on a single sheet and appeared in the *Post* as an inside feature in July 1943. The fire, which consumed his studio, also destroyed the drawings he'd made of his visit to the White House for a *Post* feature to be called "So You Want to See the President!" Fortunately, White House staff welcomed him back for four more days of sketching to replace the works he'd lost; the feature was published on November 13, 1943. Rockwell sketched the White House reporters relaxing on the leather sofa and the news photographers waiting outside the Executive Wing. He drew Senator Connally of Texas and Senator Austin of Vermont deep in conversation on an executive sofa. He used his Vermont neighbors to stand in as Secret Service agents because he wasn't permitted to sketch the actual agents for security reasons. On a coatrack hangs the President's gas mask, and among the fedoras, military hats, and berets sits a very British black top hat.

RIGHT:

So You Want to See the President!
"'Credentials, please,' says MP at White House gate."
First published in *The Saturday Evening Post,* November 13, 1943

BELOW:

So You Want to See the President!
"Landmark of Executive Wing lobby—a carved round table of Philippine mahogany. Hanging from it, reporters' coats and two Secret Service men."
First published in *The Saturday Evening Post,* November 13, 1943

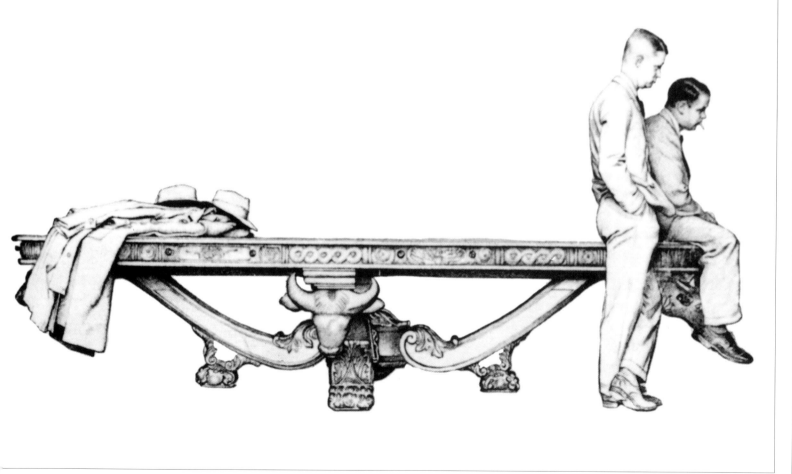

TOP:

So You Want to See the President!

"The guardian of the visitors' coat rack hands a departing guest his hat."

First published in *The Saturday Evening Post*, November 13, 1943

BOTTOM:

So You Want to See the President!

"Correspondents sprint for telephones with an Early communiqué."

First published in *The Saturday Evening Post*, November 13, 1943

RIGHT:
So You Want to See the President!
*"Genial 'Pa' Watson opens the big door and
says, 'Step this way. The president will see
you now.'"*
First published in *The Saturday Evening Post*,
November 13, 1943

BELOW:
**So You Want to See the
President!**
*"The President's gas mask, ready
to grab."*
First published in *The Saturday
Evening Post*, November 13, 1943

ABOVE:
So You Want to See the President!
*"Photographers waiting outside the Executive
Wing entrance for a newsworthy face. Your
credentials are checked again behind that door
by Secret Service."*
First published in *The Saturday Evening Post*,
November 13, 1943

Norman Rockwell Visits a Ration Board
Oil on canvas
First published in *The Saturday Evening Post,* July 15, 1944

Eventually this new journalistic style of painting became a series for the *Post* called Norman Rockwell Visits..., which featured a major oil painting and accompanying sketches from a visit Rockwell would make for the *Post* to a particular location. His first visit was to a wartime ration board in July 1943. Rockwell painted himself waiting and watching as a fellow Vermonter addresses the seven-member board. It was a familiar scene in wartime America. Across the United States, wartime ration boards had to decide how the rationed goods were to be distributed within their communities. Rockwell sketched other Vermont citizens waiting with their ration cards in hand. When the feature was published in the *Post* the individual sketches were lined up below the oil painting, as if these Vermonters were also waiting to have their say before the board.

In November 1944, Rockwell painted citizens of the United States at the polls through sketches and a *Post* cover featuring a character named Wimple. This feature was humorous and less journalistic than the Norman Rockwell Visits... series had been. In a lighthearted manner it depicts the democratic process in 1944. Wimple's friends and family try to influence Wimple before he casts his vote. Rockwell drew scenes of Wimple approaching the voting booth, voting, and eventually celebrating his candidate's election. Of course, the victory Wimple is celebrating belonged to President Franklin D. Roosevelt, who was elected to an unprecedented fourth term in 1944.

Rockwell returned to the pure realism of the Norman Rockwell Visits... series after the war, when he visited a midwestern country newspaper. In the main oil painting, Rockwell depicted himself entering the newspaper's office, where the editor, Jack Blanton, types out a story on a manual typewriter. To accompany the oil painting Rockwell sketched the linotype operator, the proofreader, and the editor

Which One?
(*also* Man in Voting Booth)
First published on the cover of
The Saturday Evening Post,
November 4, 1944

doing their jobs. And if modern viewers need more evidence that times have changed, they need only look at the intensive labor that was once involved in the process. The printer's young helper is shown dropping a hand-set grocery advertisement in one sketch; in another, he is melting down the used type in a potbellied stove in preparation for the next edition.

Rockwell didn't sketch an actual maternity-ward waiting room for the drawing that appeared in the *Post* in 1946 (page 100). Nonetheless, his depiction documents in a humorous way how maternity waiting rooms have changed over the years. American maternity waiting rooms may never have been full of so many expectant fathers pacing, wringing their hands, chewing

their fingernails, and anxiously ripping up paper as depicted by Rockwell, but it was the norm for fathers of the middle decades of the twentieth century to wait in such rooms to hear the news from the doctor. Today most fathers witness the birth of their children at the mother's side, right in the delivery room.

"Norman Rockwell Visits a Country School," published in November 1946, shows the challenges faced by the one teacher at Oak Mountain School in Carroll County, Georgia. The main oil painting features the teacher reading to her pupils, who are gathered around the potbellied stove. Many of her students are not wearing shoes. To accompany the painting, Rockwell sketched the exterior of the weather-beaten school, extracurricular activities, a spelling bee, and the teacher facing the three-man school board. Rockwell set out to paint southern poverty and one teacher's heroic efforts to educate disadvantaged children, but no mention is made of the African-American experience in the South. Middle America in the mid-1940s wasn't yet prepared to face the inequities fostered by racial intolerance and segregation.

ABOVE, LEFT:
Norman Rockwell Visits a Country Editor
"No rural weekly is complete without a poet. Blanton hearkens for throbs of genius as Mrs. Ruth Owens recites a few choice strophes."
Pencil or charcoal on paper
10.5 × 10 inches (26.5 × 25.5cm)
First published in *The Saturday Evening Post,* May 25, 1946

ABOVE, RIGHT:
Norman Rockwell Visits a Country Editor
"Practical man. Literary flights, like Blanton editorial or Ruth Owens sonnet, are cast in metal form by Paul Nipps, linotyper."
First published in *The Saturday Evening Post,* May 25, 1946

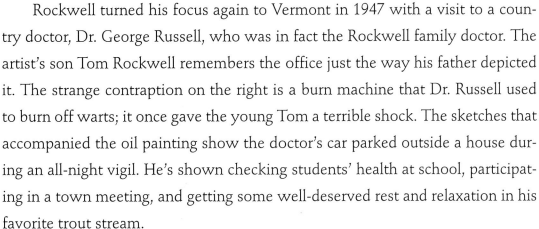

Rockwell turned his focus again to Vermont in 1947 with a visit to a country doctor, Dr. George Russell, who was in fact the Rockwell family doctor. The artist's son Tom Rockwell remembers the office just the way his father depicted it. The strange contraption on the right is a burn machine that Dr. Russell used to burn off warts; it once gave the young Tom a terrible shock. The sketches that accompanied the oil painting show the doctor's car parked outside a house during an all-night vigil. He's shown checking students' health at school, participating in a town meeting, and getting some well-deserved rest and relaxation in his favorite trout stream.

The last of the Norman Rockwell Visits... series depicts a county agent in Jay County, Indiana. Rockwell painted the agent examining a young 4-H member's cow. The accompanying sketches show the agent addressing fellow Rotarians, analyzing soil, and surveying fields. The agent is also shown culling a hen, tasting homemade pie, and losing at a family game of checkers. The county agent grouping appeared in the *Post* in July 1948.

ABOVE, LEFT:
Norman Rockwell Visits a Country Editor
"Thursday, day of issue. Blondie stacks; Blanton checks for errors; and Higgens stamps on subscribers' addresses."
Charcoal or pencil on poster board
20 × 50 inches (51 × 127cm)
First published in *The Saturday Evening Post*, May 25, 1946

ABOVE, RIGHT:
Norman Rockwell Visits a Country Editor
"After each edition is published, Dickie and Blondie melt down the type for re-use in Nipps' linotype."
First published in *The Saturday Evening Post*, May 25, 1946

ABOVE:
Maternity Waiting Room
First published in *The Saturday Evening Post*, July 13, 1946

LEFT:
Norman Rockwell Visits a Country Doctor
    *"A quiet evening unbroken by sick calls is a rarity: so is
    a night's unbroken sleep."*
First published in *The Saturday Evening Post*, April 12, 1947

RIGHT:
Norman Rockwell Visits a Country Doctor
    *"Consultation. It may be bad news: 'One more day like
    this and you can go back to school.'"*
First published in *The Saturday Evening Post*, April 12, 1947

BELOW:
Norman Rockwell Visits a Country Doctor
"A school doctor. He treats all ages—from portal to portal, a wag said."
First published in *The Saturday Evening Post*, April 12, 1947

ABOVE:
Norman Rockwell Visits a Country Doctor
Oil on canvas
32 × 60 inches (81 × 152.5cm)
First published in *The Saturday Evening Post*, April 12, 1947

BELOW:
Norman Rockwell Visits a Country Doctor
"The waiting room. The office is part of his fine old colonial house on main street."
First published in *The Saturday Evening Post*, April 12, 1947

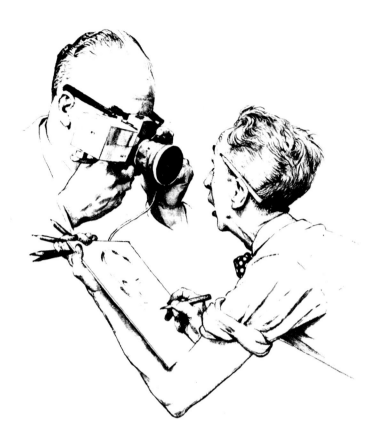

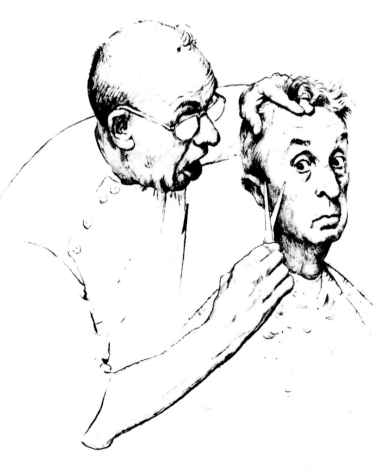

ABOVE:
I Paint the Candidates
(*also* Norman Having Picture Taken)
Ink wash and pencil on paper
11.5 × 12.5 inches (29 × 31.5cm)
First published in *Look*, October 20, 1964

OPPOSITE:
Elect Casey
Oil on canvas
52 × 42 inches (132 × 106.5cm)
First published on the cover of *The Saturday
Evening Post*, November 8, 1958

ABOVE:
I Paint the Candidates
*"I positively know who I'm voting for, but
if anyone can guess, I've failed as an old
political art pro."*
First published in *Look*, October 20, 1964

LEFT:
I Paint the Candidates
*"Before a painter goes to the White
House, he had better get a haircut and
listen to an expert explain politics."*
Charcoal
11 × 10 inches (28 × 25.5cm)
First published in *Look*, October 20, 1964

DO UNTO OTHERS
AS YOU WOULD HAVE THEM
DO UNTO YOU

CHAPTER FOUR

An Artist of the Twentieth Century

1960–1978

Rockwell grieved deeply after Mary's death, but he also continued to paint. His work gave structure to his life, even during such times of crisis.

In 1960 Rockwell painted the portraits of presidential candidates John F. Kennedy and Richard M. Nixon. Rockwell's autobiography, *My Adventures as an Illustrator,* was also published that year.

In the spring of 1961, Rockwell joined an adult education class to study poetry with Molly Punderson. She had grown up in Stockbridge and had recently retired as a literature teacher from the Milton Academy. In October 1961 Norman and Molly were married.

The *Post* published "Golden Rule" in 1961, which featured depictions of people from around the world in native dress. Its message was one of tolerance. Rockwell painted the biblical phrase "Do unto others as you would have them do unto you" across the bottom of the painting.

Norman and Molly Rockwell traveled to India, Cairo, and Yugoslavia for the *Post,* and Rockwell painted the portraits of Nehru, Nasser, and Tito. Rockwell's last *Post* cover

Golden Rule
Oil on canvas
44.5 × 39.5 inches
(113.5 × 100.5cm)
First published on the cover of
The Saturday Evening Post,
April 1, 1961

was published in 1963. It was a reprint of the Kennedy portrait from 1960, which was published again after the president's assassination.

In the early 1960s, however, the *Post* was beginning to fail. The magazine was redesigned in 1961, and in 1962 the editors decided to use mostly portraits or photographs on the covers. Rockwell's human interest covers were no longer in demand. Instead, the editors sent Rockwell around the world doing portraits of international figures. The *Post* published his portraits of Nehru and Nasser but decided not to publish his portrait of Tito. Unhappy with the direction in which the magazine was taking him, Rockwell left the *Post* in 1963. He began to do work for *Look* magazine and returned to using his art as a form of reportage, which he hadn't done for many years. His new focus reflected both the magazine's and the decade's concern for social and political issues.

In 1969 the *Post* ceased publication. When it was revived in 1971 Rockwell posed for a photograph beside a *Post* newsboy, but he graciously declined an invitation to do illustrations for the magazine.

Rockwell's first painting for *Look* magazine was published in January 1964. It featured a child making her way to school. This was not an unexpected theme for Rockwell, and indeed was one that he had painted in the early days of his career. This time, however, instead of a cute dog trotting by her side, the little girl is escorted by U.S. marshals. A tomato has been thrown at her and its pulverized, blood red remains are prominent against an ugly wall of racial hatred. Civil rights had become a mainstream issue in the 1960s. The combined effect of *Look* magazine's style and the general public's growing awareness of the civil rights movement enabled Rockwell to show the hardships brought on by racial intolerance.

Rockwell painted the murder of three civil rights workers in Mississippi (pages 108 and 109). A white worker is shown holding his dying black friend as menacing shadows approach. Another civil rights worker lies dying on the ground. *Look* accepted the color study for publication instead of the more detailed finished painting because the editors thought the study was more powerful.

Rockwell's third wife, Molly, encouraged him to paint his political convictions. Rockwell was quoted in 1971 as saying:

> *The Marines had me down at Quantico. I was supposed to do a portrait of*
> *a Marine in Vietnam kneeling over to help a wounded villager and love shining*
> *in their eyes....I thought about it a lot and [Molly] said, "You can't do that and*

The Problem We All Live With
(*also* Walking to School; Schoolgirl with U.S. Marshals)
Oil on canvas
36 × 58 inches (91.5 × 147.5cm)
First published in *Look*, January 14, 1964

OPPOSITE:
Southern Justice
(*also* Murder in Mississippi)
Oil on board
15 × 12.75 inches (40.5 × 32.5cm)
First published in *Look*, June 29, 1965
(Note that the color study was published
in preference to the final painting. Both the
Look editors and Rockwell felt the study
more vividly portrayed the emotional
impact of the event.)

ABOVE:
Southern Justice
(*also* Murder in Mississippi)
Oil on canvas
53 × 42 inches (134.5 × 106.5cm)
Unpublished version, 1965

BELOW:
Southern Justice
Pencil on board
15.5 × 15 inches (39.5 × 38cm)
Unpublished version, study for "Southern
Justice" (*also* Murder in Mississippi), 1965

New Kids in the Neighborhood
(*also* Moving In)
Oil on canvas
36.5 × 57.5 inches (91.5 × 146cm)
First published in *Look*, May 16, 1967

you know you can't....I don't think we're helping the Vietnamese people lead better lives, do you?"

In the late 1960s Rockwell painted "Blood Brothers" for the Congress of Racial Equality. In this painting two U.S. soldiers, one black and the other white, lie dying side by side. Their blood flows together on the dry soil.

Rockwell painted the curiosity and potential felt by young people when a black family moved into a white suburb. Will the children close their ears to the racism of their parents and play ball? Rockwell saw hope in the young people of his day.

Rockwell documented this optimism for *Look* when he visited young Americans working for the Peace Corps in Ethiopia, India, and Columbia in 1966. The young adults are shown sharing their knowledge to benefit the lives of their hosts. He also painted the profile of John F. Kennedy, who established the Peace Corps in 1961, leading a group of young people who are also shown in profile. To ensure the painting's authenticity, Rockwell used models of people who had served overseas with the Peace Corps.

Rockwell also documented the United States' race to the moon with a number of paintings for *Look.* He visited NASA several times to record astronauts and their space suits, the Apollo 11 space team, and eventually men walking on the moon and leaving their footsteps behind. The artist, who as a young boy had waved self-consciously from the back seat of an early automobile, would wave from aboard the Apollo space module more than sixty years later. While always reflecting the artist's experiences in life, Rockwell's art also recorded pivotal moments in world history.

He also renewed his relationship with *McCall's* and did a number of illustrations and a cover for that magazine. He and Molly traveled extensively, both for *Look* magazine and for pleasure. While they traveled she took many pho-

Peace Corps
(*also* JFK's Bold Legacy)
Oil on canvas
45.5 × 36.5 inches (115.5 x 92.5cm)
First published on the cover of *Look,* June 14, 1966

The Right to Know
Oil on canvas
29 × 54 inches (73.5 × 137cm)
First published in *Look*,
August 20, 1968

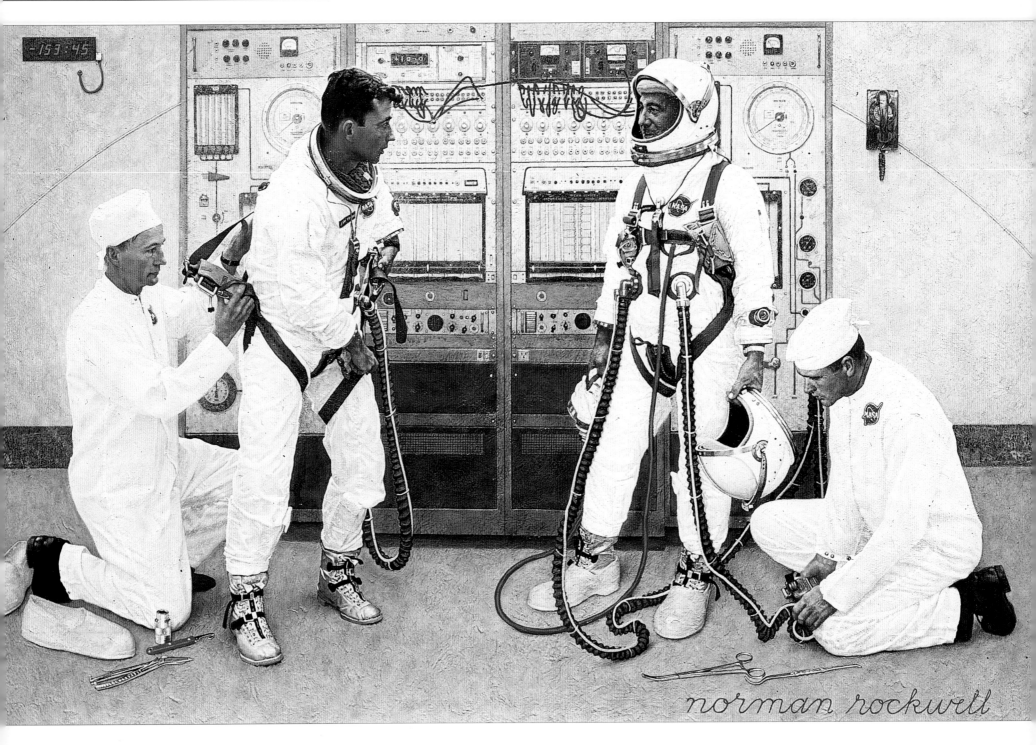

The Longest Step
(*also* Grissom and Young Suiting Up)
Oil on canvas
33 × 52.375 inches (84 × 133cm)
First published in *Look,* April 20, 1965

tographs, which Rockwell would refer to when he returned to the studio. In 1967 they collaborated on the children's book *Willie Was Different.*

Toward the end of his life, Rockwell received many honors in recognition of his truly remarkable career. In 1977 President Gerald R. Ford awarded Rockwell the Presidential Medal of Freedom for his "vivid and affectionate portraits of our country."

Norman Rockwell died on November 8, 1978, at his home in Stockbridge, Massachusetts, leaving his wife, Molly, three sons, and seven grandchildren.

Apollo and Beyond
  (*also* Apollo 2 Space Team)
  Oil on canvas
  28.5 × 66 inches (72.5 × 167.5cm)
  First published in *Look*, July 15, 1969

RIGHT:

The Final Impossibility: Man's Tracks on the Moon
(*also* Two Men on the Moon)
Oil on canvas
42.5 × 61.5 inches (108 × 156cm)
First published in *Look*, December 30, 1969

BELOW:

Man on the Moon
(*also* Portrait of an Astronaut)
Oil on canvas
10 × 8.35 inches (25.5 × 21cm)
First published in *Look*, January 10, 1967

ABOVE:

Tranquillity

(*also* From Concord to Tranquillity)
First used as a Boy Scouts of America calendar illustration, 1973

Picasso vs. Sargent
Oil on canvas
23 × 17 inches (58.5 × 43cm)
First published in *Look*, January 11, 1966

An Artist of the Twentieth Century

Norman Rockwell's more than four thousand illustrations, which include covers, advertisements, and story illustrations, reflect the times he lived through. From the early automobile to the early airplane and from hay wagons to man's footprints on the moon, Rockwell witnessed a great deal of history unfold and documented his particular view of the United States—and the world—for publication.

Rockwell's longevity, remarkable talents, and sympathetic outlook resulted in the creation of a comprehensive visual commentary on a changing America. The importance he placed on authenticity enables successive generations to see details that impart a greater understanding of the periods of history he observed. Moreover, Rockwell's work continues to welcome generation after generation of viewers to share in the humor and sensitivity of an artist who had a great deal to say about his country and his times.

Liberty Bell
(*also* Celebration)
Oil on canvas
45 × 33 inches (114.5 × 84cm)
First published on the cover of
American Artist, July 1976

Photography Credits

All artwork courtesy of the Norman Rockwell Museum at Stockbridge, Stockbridge MA, except as noted below:

Rockwell Museum, Corning, New York: 19 bottom

Wadsworth Atheneum, Hartford, Connecticut. Gift of Kenneth Stuart: 30